Microsoft

Outlook 98

Field
Guide

PUBLISHED BY
Microsoft Press
A Division of Microsoft Corporation
One Microsoft Way
Redmond, Washington 98052-6399

Copyright © 1998 by Stephen L. Nelson, Inc.

Library of Congress Cataloging-in-Publication Data
Nelson, Stephen L., 1959-
    Microsoft Outlook 98 Field Guide / Stephen L. Nelson.
       p.   cm.
    Includes index.
    ISBN 1-57231-728-0
    1. Microsoft Outlook.   2. Time management--Computer programs.
    3. Personal information management--Computer programs.   I. Title.
    HD69.T54N453   1998
    005.369--dc21   98-11185
                                                             CIP

Printed and bound in the United States of America.

    2 3 4 5 6 7 8 9   MLML   3 2 1 0 9 8

Distributed to the book trade in Canada by Macmillan of Canada,
a division of Canada Publishing Corporation.

A CIP catalogue record for this book is available from the British Library.

Microsoft Press books are available through booksellers and distributors
worldwide. For further information about international editions, contact your
local Microsoft Corporation office, or contact Microsoft Press International
directly at fax (425) 936-7329. Visit our Web site at mspress.microsoft.com.

Acquisitions Editor: Susanne M. Forderer
Project Editor: Anne Taussig

Microsoft
Outlook 98

Field
Guide

Stephen L. Nelson   **Microsoft** Press

The Microsoft Outlook 98 Field Guide *is divided into five sections. These sections are designed to help you find the information you need quickly.*

1 Environment

Terms and ideas you'll want to know to get the most out of Microsoft Outlook. All the basic parts of Outlook are shown and explained. The emphasis here is on quick answers, but many topics are cross-referenced so that you can find out more if you want to.

Diagrams of key components, with quick definitions, cross-referenced to more complete information.

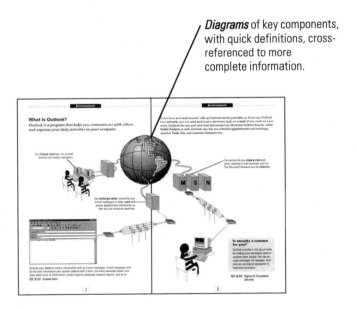

Tips

Watch for these as you use this Field Guide. They'll point out helpful hints and let you know what to watch for.

15 | Outlook A to Z

An alphabetic list of commands, tasks, terms, and procedures.

Definitions of key concepts and terms, and examples showing you why you should know them.

Step-by-step guides to performing most Outlook tasks.

Cross-references to related topics.

159 | Troubleshooting

A guide to common problems—how to avoid them, and what to do when they occur.

169 | Quick Reference

Useful indexes, including a full list of menu commands, shortcut keys, and more.

187 | Index

A complete reference to all elements of the Field Guide.

Introduction

In the real world, you need
practical solutions. Fast.
This Field Guide provides
just these sorts of lightning-
quick answers. But take two
minutes now and read the
Introduction. It explains
how this unusual little
book works.

What Is a Field Guide?

Sometime during grade school, my parents gave me a field guide to North American birds. With its visual approach, its maps, and its numerous illustrations, that guide delivered hours of enjoyment. The book also helped me better understand and more fully appreciate the birds in my neighborhood. And the small book fit neatly in my backpack. But I'm getting off the track.

This book works in the same way as that field guide. It organizes information visually with numerous illustrations. And it does this in a way that helps you more easily understand and enjoy working with Microsoft Outlook 98. For new users, the Field Guide provides the essential information necessary to start using Outlook. But the Field Guide isn't only for beginners. For experienced users, the Field Guide provides concise, easy-to-find descriptions of Outlook tasks, terms, and techniques.

When You Have a Question

Let me explain then how to find the information you need. If Outlook is new to you, you'll usually want to flip first to the Environment section, which is really a visual index. You find the picture that shows what you want to do or the task you have a question about. If you want to know how to send e-mail messages, you flip to pages 4 and 5, which talk about how you send an e-mail message over a network using Outlook.

Next you read the captions that describe the parts of the picture. Say, for example, that you want to attach a file to send along with your message. On page 4, there's a caption that describes what message attachments are.

You'll notice that some captions use **boldface** terms or are followed by additional boldface terms. These provide more information related to the caption's contents by referring to entries in the second section, Outlook A to Z.

Outlook A to Z is a dictionary containing right around 200 entries that define terms and describe tasks. (After you've worked with Outlook a bit or if you're already an experienced user, you'll often be able to turn directly to this section.) So if you have just read the caption in the Environment section that talks about message attachments, you'll see the term **item** in boldface, indicating a cross-reference. If you don't know what an Outlook item is, you can flip to the Items entry in Outlook A to Z.

When an entry in Outlook A to Z appears as a term within another entry, I'll often **boldface** it the first time it appears in that entry. For example, as part of describing what an Outlook item is, I might tell you that an appointment is an example of an Outlook item. In this case, the word **appointment** appears in bold letters—alerting you to the presence of another entry explaining appointments and how you create them using Outlook's Calendar. If you don't understand the term or want to do a bit of brushing up, you can flip to the Appointment entry for more information.

When You Have a Problem

The third section, Troubleshooting, describes problems that new and casual users of Outlook often encounter. Following each problem description, I list one or more solutions you can employ to fix the problem.

When You Wonder About a Command

The Quick Reference at the end of the Field Guide describes the Outlook menu commands and toolbar buttons. If you want to know what a specific command does, turn to the Quick Reference. Don't forget about the Index either. You can look there to find all references in this book to any single topic.

Conventions Used Here

I have developed a few conventions to make using this book easier for you. Rather than use wordy phrases such as "Activate the File menu, and then choose the Print command" to describe how you choose a menu command, I'm just going to say, "Choose the File menu's Print command."

Finally, I want to let you know about a couple of conventions I used when creating the figures for this book so that you won't get confused if the figures you see here look a little different than what you see on your screen. When I installed Outlook to create the figures for this book, I didn't upgrade from Outlook 97. This is why my Outlook Bar's buttons are called Outlook Shortcuts, My Shortcuts, and Other Shortcuts. If you upgraded from Outlook 97, your buttons may be called Outlook, Mail, and Other. But you have pretty much the same icons in each group as I do. The computer I used for creating the figures for this book is also part of a network. So I installed the Corporate or Workgroup version of Outlook. If you installed the Internet Only or No E-Mail version of Outlook, your Address Book might look a little different and you will have fewer options in some dialog boxes. Finally, I performed the full installation of Outlook so that I could tell you about some of the features in that version. If you installed the Standard or Minimal version, you might not have all of the features I talk about.

Environment

Need to get oriented
quickly? Then the
Environment is the place
to start. It defines
the key terms you'll need
to know and the core
ideas you should
understand as you
begin exploring
Microsoft Outlook 98.

What Is Outlook?

Outlook is a program that helps you communicate with others and organize your daily activities on your computer.

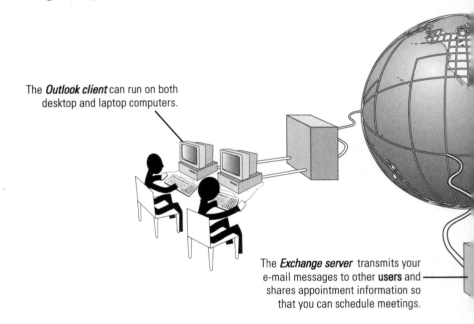

The *Outlook client* can run on both desktop and laptop computers.

The *Exchange server* transmits your e-mail messages to other **users** and shares appointment information so that you can schedule meetings.

Outlook uses *forms* to collect information such as e-mail messages. E-mail messages may be the only information your system collects with a form, but many networks collect and store other kinds of information: project reports, employee expense reports, and so on.

SEE ALSO   Custom Form

If you have an e-mail account with an **Internet service provider,** or if you use Outlook on a **network,** you can send and receive electronic mail, or **e-mail.** If you work on a network, Outlook lets you post and read information on electronic bulletin boards, called **Public Folders,** as well. Outlook also lets you schedule **appointments** and meetings, monitor **Tasks** lists, and maintain **Contacts** lists.

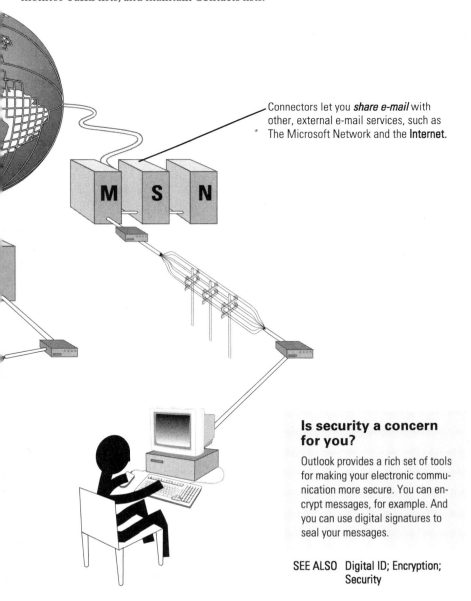

Connectors let you *share e-mail* with other, external e-mail services, such as The Microsoft Network and the **Internet.**

Is security a concern for you?

Outlook provides a rich set of tools for making your electronic communication more secure. You can encrypt messages, for example. And you can use digital signatures to seal your messages.

SEE ALSO   Digital ID; Encryption; Security

Sending Your Messages

With Outlook, you can easily send e-mail messages to other network users or over the Internet.

Send your message by clicking the Send toolbar button when you finish the message.

Click To or Cc to see the **Address Book.** It lists the names of everyone in your organization so that you can easily find and use their addresses to send messages.
SEE ALSO   Blind Carbon Copy; Copy; Distribution List; E-Mail Name

Type the *message body* into the main part of the Message form.

Message attachments let you send a file or another Outlook **item** with your message.

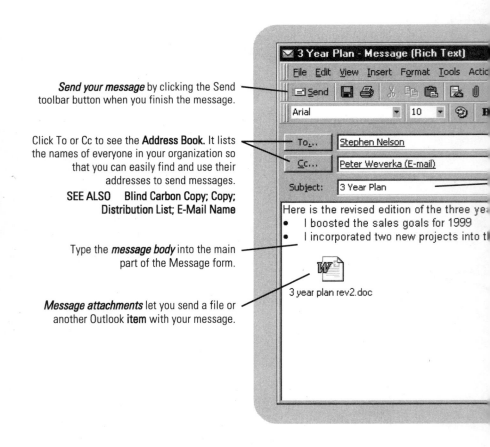

To create an e-mail **message,** you use the **Message form** to name the **recipient,** identify the message **subject,** and then type the body of your message. While text-only messages are probably most common, you can also use Outlook to e-mail **files.**

Add *formatting* to your message by using the **toolbar.**
SEE ALSO   Alignment; Bullets; Character Formatting; Font

Identify the *message subject* by entering text in the **Subject** box.

The *Message form* window provides input blanks you use to write your message.
SEE ALSO   Form

Reading Your Messages

Outlook makes it easy to organize and read your incoming messages. The Inbox is Outlook's incoming message center.

The *Folder List* displays your Personal Folders and any of the Public Folders available for messages. Double-click the **Inbox** folder to view incoming messages.

Click one of the icons on the **Outlook Bar** to move to that **folder**.

The *message header* identifies who sent the message, the message recipients, the message **subject,** and the date and time the message was sent.

Outlook uses **folders** to organize messages. **Personal Folders** store the messages you receive and copies of the messages you send. **Public Folders** store the **posts** that you want to make available to other **users** on a network. When you find the folder with the message you want to read, double-click the message to read it.

The *information viewer* shows the messages in a folder grouped and sorted any way you want. Double-click a message to read it.

SEE ALSO Grouping Items; Read and Unread Messages; Sorting

A *message* appears in its own window so you can read it easily. The Message window also provides **toolbar** buttons that you can use to print, delete, **reply** to, or **forward** the message.

Sent: Thu 02/12/98 12:18 PM

ng with the project team?

Do you need help with your messages?

If you receive a large number of messages, Outlook provides two useful tools to help you manage and monitor your incoming messages. The **Rules Wizard** alerts you to messages you receive and also automatically moves, replies to, or forwards messages. The **Out Of Office Assistant** automatically replies to messages when you're away from your computer.

How the Calendar Works

Outlook helps you maintain an appointment calendar and a task list.

Click one of the icons on the **Outlook Bar** to move to that **folder.**

You can tell Outlook to display *Reminders* that alert you to upcoming appointments and **events.**

Appointments are entered in time-slots in your Calendar.
SEE ALSO Private Appointments and Tasks; Recurring Appointment

You use the **Calendar** to schedule your time commitments: meetings, **appointments,** deadlines, and so forth. You use the **TaskPad** to keep track of the **tasks** you need to complete.

Meetings are easier to schedule because Outlook does the work of finding the earliest open time-slot that the meeting attendees have in common.

SEE ALSO   Busy Time; Delegate Access; Permission

The *TaskPad* is a compact version of the Tasks list that lets you keep track of the individual tasks that you need to complete.

SEE ALSO   Recurring Task

Keeping Track of Your Contacts

The Contacts folder lets you keep records of business and personal contacts.

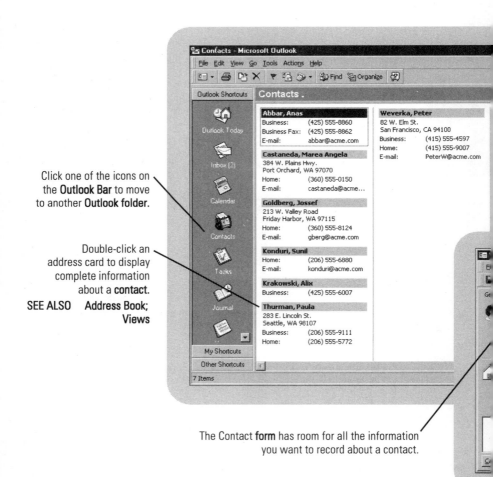

Click one of the icons on the **Outlook Bar** to move to another **Outlook folder.**

Double-click an address card to display complete information about a **contact.**

SEE ALSO   Address Book; Views

The Contact **form** has room for all the information you want to record about a contact.

You can use the **Contacts** list to keep track of the names, mailing addresses, phone numbers, and e-mail addresses of all your customers, vendors, contractors, friends, family members, and acquaintances. You can display and view information about your contacts in a list or as alphabetized index cards.

Click a letter button to display the cards of contacts whose names begin with a certain letter.

Use this tab to enter **NetMeeting** information for a contact.

Keeping a Journal and Writing Notes

The Journal folder lets you automatically track messages, tasks, and even Microsoft Office files. Notes are handy ways to post reminders.

Click one of the icons on the **Outlook Bar** to move to that **folder**.

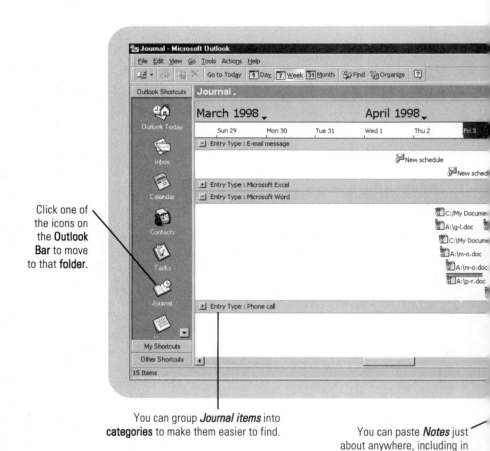

You can group *Journal items* into categories to make them easier to find.

You can paste *Notes* just about anywhere, including in e-mail messages.

Use the **Journal** to automatically maintain a running list of all the messages you send and receive, notes you write, tasks you work on, and **Microsoft Word,** Microsoft Excel, and Microsoft PowerPoint files you create. Or add manual Journal entries for activities you do away from your computer—for letters you write or projects you work on. View your Journal events against a timeline or in a list. Create **Notes** to paste on your desktop or in messages, and color-code them for easy filing.

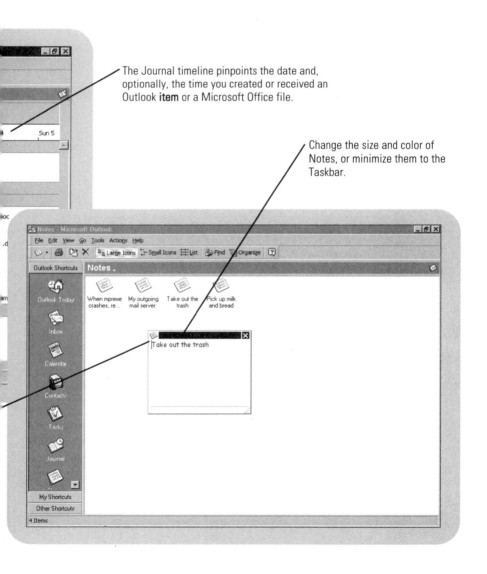

The Journal timeline pinpoints the date and, optionally, the time you created or received an Outlook **item** or a Microsoft Office file.

Change the size and color of Notes, or minimize them to the Taskbar.

Microsoft Outlook

A to Z

Maybe it's not a jungle out there. But you'll still want to keep a field guide close at hand. Microsoft Outlook A to Z, which starts on the next page, lists in alphabetic order the tools, terms, and techniques you'll need to know.

Actions

Within Outlook, the term *action* can refer to two separate things. *Actions* is the name of a menu with unique commands for working with a folder's items. For example, when the **Inbox** is displayed, the Actions menu provides commands for working with messages. And when the **Tasks** folder is displayed, the Actions menu provides commands for working with tasks. (By the way, because the **Outlook folders** offer such similar menus, once you learn how to work with one folder, you'll find it very easy to work with the others.)

The term *actions* also refers to automatic responses that you tell Outlook to perform in certain situations. For example, you can tell Outlook to open the next **message** in the **Inbox** information viewer after you delete the current message. You can set controls for most actions on the various tabs of the Options dialog box, which you open by choosing the Tools menu's Options command.

SEE ALSO Rules Wizard; Quick Reference: Actions Menu Commands

Active Desktop

Microsoft Internet Explorer 4 lets you turn the regular Windows desktop into an Active Desktop. What this means, essentially, is that you can display web pages or portions of web pages on your desktop. If you want to know more about Active Desktop, you may want to refer to either the Internet Explorer's online help information or a book about Internet Explorer 4.

Address Book

Outlook provides a tool called the Address Book that you can use to find the name and address information you need to send e-mail. The Address Book lists all the people you've described using the **Contacts** folder, all the people that appear on the **Global Address List** (if your computer is connected to a network that includes Microsoft **Exchange Server**), and all the people you've described using a **Personal Address Book**. In some cases, the Address Book even provides access to other lists of e-mail addresses, too.

Adding E-Mail Names to an Address Book List

If you have already received a **message** from someone, it's easy to add this person's name to your Contacts folder or to your Personal Address Book. Just display the message that the person sent you, and then right-click the sender's name in the message header. To add the sender's name and address to your Contacts folder, choose the shortcut menu's Add To Contacts command and enter information about the sender. To add the sender to your Personal Address Book, choose the shortcut menu's Add To Personal Address Book command. In the future, you will be able to use the Address Book to retrieve the sender's address whenever you send a message.

If you want to add the e-mail address and name of someone from whom you haven't received a message to your Address Book, you can add a contact to the Contacts folder by displaying the Contacts folder and clicking the New Contact button. If you're not using the Contacts folder and are instead using a Personal Address Book, you can use the Address Book to add an e-mail name and address. To do this, click the Address Book toolbar button to display the Address Book and click New Entry to add a new entry to an Address Book list. Then select the type of entry you want to add and the Address Book list to which you want to add it. Enter the person's address using the various tabs of the dialog box that Outlook provides.

Using Address Book Names to Send E-Mail

Typically, you use the information in the Address Book to e-mail someone a message. To do this, click To or Cc on the Message form. Outlook displays the Select Names dialog box.

Click the down arrow in the Show Names From The drop-down list to specify whether you want to see the names of people in your Contacts folder or on some other list such as the Global Address List or your Personal Address Book. Then to select someone in the Address Book, double-click a name to add it to the Message Recipients list.

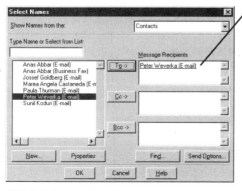

After the names of everyone who should receive the message have been added to the Message Recipients list, click OK.

SEE ALSO   Distribution List

17

Administrator

If your computer is connected to a network, your administrator is the person whose job it is to take care of the network. This person is probably the same one who told you about Outlook and set up your **mailbox.** You should try to learn who the network administrator is if you don't already know. If you have problems sending a **message** to someone else over the network, you can probably get help from the administrator.

Alignment

You can usually change the alignment of a paragraph or paragraphs in the Message form. To do this, simply click the paragraph you want to align (or to align several paragraphs at once, click in one and drag over the others) and then click the Align Left, Center, or Align Right toolbar buttons.

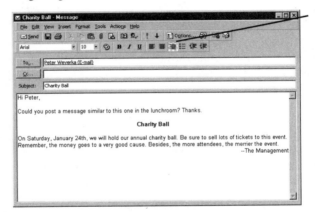

The faces of the Alignment toolbar buttons show how they align text.

Annual Event SEE Event

Appointment

Outlook lets you record appointments in the **Calendar.** To add an appointment, click the Calendar icon on the **Outlook Bar.** Then click the appointment date on the **Date Navigator.**

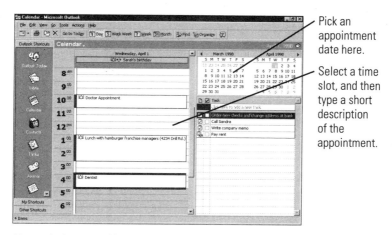

Pick an appointment date here.

Select a time slot, and then type a short description of the appointment.

Alternatively, to provide more detailed information about an appointment you're adding, just double-click any block of time. Or click the New Appointment toolbar button. Then use the Appointment dialog box to describe the appointment in detail.

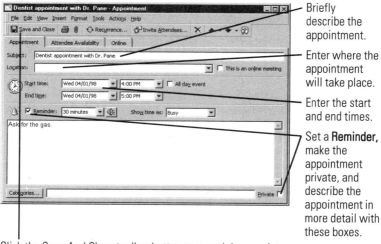

Briefly describe the appointment.

Enter where the appointment will take place.

Enter the start and end times.

Set a **Reminder,** make the appointment private, and describe the appointment in more detail with these boxes.

Click the Save And Close toolbar button to record the appointment.

SEE ALSO   Recurring Appointment

Archive

Outlook allows you to create archives. An archive is a portion of an existing **Outlook folder** that is stored in a separate file, which is called an archive. For example, suppose you had two years' worth of scheduling information, for 1997 and 1998, in an existing file. You could create an archive for the 1997 scheduling information. This way, the information no longer appears in your regular schedule—and Outlook runs faster—although the information remains available in the archive in case you ever need it.

Outlook will automatically archive items in the **Calendar, Inbox, Journal,** and Sent Items folders. What's more, you can tell Outlook to archive items in other Outlook folders, or you can turn off AutoArchive altogether. (You can't archive items in the **Contacts** folder because contact items usually don't become obsolete just because they're old.) You can also tell AutoArchive to delete old items instead of archiving them. To use AutoArchive, first you must enable it and then you must set AutoArchive options for each folder you want to archive.

Enabling AutoArchive

To enable AutoArchive, choose the Tools menu's Options command, click the Other tab, and then click AutoArchive.

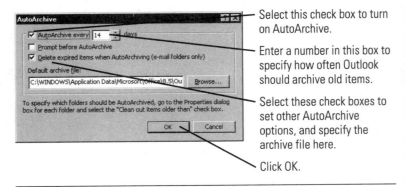

Select this check box to turn on AutoArchive.

Enter a number in this box to specify how often Outlook should archive old items.

Select these check boxes to set other AutoArchive options, and specify the archive file here.

Click OK.

Setting AutoArchive Folder Options

You set AutoArchive options individually for each folder you want to archive. To set options for the **Tasks** folder, for example, right-click the Tasks icon on the **Outlook Bar** and then choose the shortcut menu's Properties command. When Outlook displays the Tasks Properties dialog box, click the AutoArchive tab.

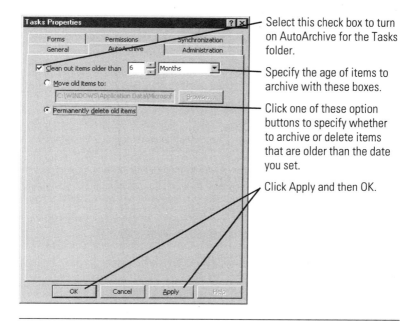

Select this check box to turn on AutoArchive for the Tasks folder.

Specify the age of items to archive with these boxes.

Click one of these option buttons to specify whether to archive or delete items that are older than the date you set.

Click Apply and then OK.

Creating Archives Manually

To create Outlook archives manually, choose the File menu's Archive command. When Outlook displays the Archive dialog box, specify what you want to name the archive file, where you want the file stored, and what you want to use as a cutoff date.

Items older than this date go into the archive file; everything else stays with the original file.

continues

Archive *(continued)*

Retrieving Archives

To retrieve the items stored in an archive file, choose the File menu's Import And Export command. To use the Import And Export Wizard, follow these steps:

1 In the first dialog box, select Import From Another Program Or File in the list box. Then click Next.

2 In the second dialog box, select Personal Folder File (.pst) in the list box. Then click Next.

3 In the third dialog box, verify that the File To Import box shows the complete path of the archive file, which will be named archive.pst. If it doesn't, click Browse and then use the Browse dialog box to locate the archive file (which will be named archive.pst).

4 Click a button in the Options area to specify what you want Outlook to do with duplicate items. For example, click the Replace Duplicates With Items Imported option button if you want to replace items in your folders with archived items. Click the Allow Duplicates To Be Created option button if you just want to add duplicate items to your folders. Click the Do Not Import Duplicates option button if you don't want to retrieve duplicate items from the archive. Then click Next.

5 In the Import Personal Folders dialog box, select the folders from which you want to import archived items. Then indicate where Outlook should place the items you retrieve. Click Finish.

Filtering archive items

If you want to decide for yourself which items Outlook retrieves from the archive, click Filter in the Import Personal Folders dialog box. Then use the Filter dialog box to describe which items you want to retrieve.

Attachment

The term *attachment* refers to a **file** or Outlook item you attach, or stick into, another Outlook item. For example, you can attach a Microsoft Office document you're working on to a task. Or you can attach a task item to an appointment. But you probably most commonly want to attach files to e-mail **messages** or **posts.** This is a quick and inexpensive way of sharing documents with other people.

SEE ALSO   MIME; Uuencode

AutoArchive   SEE   Archive

AutoCreate

Outlook lets you automatically create new **items** by dragging an item from one folder to another. For example, if you drag a meeting request from your Inbox to the Calendar folder or a task request from your Inbox to the Tasks folder, Outlook automatically creates new calendar and task items. (In these two special cases, Outlook also sends an acceptance reply to the sender.)

SEE ALSO **Plan A Meeting Wizard**

AutoDial

If you have a modem and a phone on the same line, Outlook can dial the phone for you. In the **Contacts** folder, click the contact you want to call, and click the AutoDialer toolbar button. Outlook displays the New Call dialog box for the selected contact.

Outlook displays the name of the selected contact here.

Click Open Contact to display the Contact dialog box for the selected contact.

Click here to display all the phone numbers you've recorded for this contact.

Click here to initiate the call.

SEE ALSO **Speed Dial**

Automatic Delivery

If your computer connects to a network that includes an **Exchange server,** Outlook automatically delivers your messages. When you click the Send toolbar button in the **Message form,** the Outlook client immediately sends the message to the Exchange server. Shortly thereafter, the Exchange server sends the message to the recipient's

Outlook client. Depending on how the administrator set up the server and the client, sending messages can take a few seconds or a few minutes. If your messages aren't being delivered quickly, something is amiss. You need to have a little chat with the **administrator**.

SEE ALSO   Deferred Delivery

AutoPreview

You can preview the first few lines of all the messages in your **Inbox** information viewer without actually displaying the messages themselves. To do this, choose the View menu's AutoPreview command.

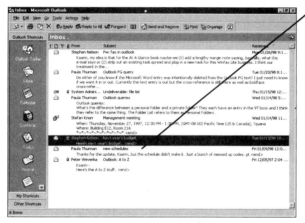

Messages appear like this when the AutoPreview view is used.

You can preview **tasks** in your Tasks list, too.

Previewing New Messages Only

You can also preview only new messages by choosing the View menu's Current View command and the Current View submenu's Messages With AutoPreview command. If you currently have this view displayed (you can tell if this is the case because Outlook displays a check mark next to this command), selecting the View menu's AutoPreview command turns AutoPreview of new messages off rather than turning AutoPreview for all messages on.

SEE ALSO   Preview Pane

AutoReply

If your office network includes an **Exchange server** and you receive office e-mail over the network, you can reply automatically to each e-mail message you receive. Automatic replies are especially handy when you want people to know that you can't reply right away because you're on vacation, traveling on business, or simply too busy to respond. To turn on AutoReply, choose the Tools menu's Out Of Office Assistant command to display the Out Of Office Assistant dialog box.

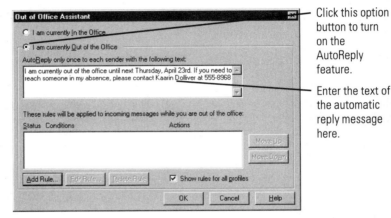

Click this option button to turn on the AutoReply feature.

Enter the text of the automatic reply message here.

AutoSignature

For years now, people—particularly Internet **users**—have been appending little snippets of text called signatures to the ends of their **e-mail messages.** Sometimes signatures list the sender's name, address, and telephone number. But they can also include quotations, art, and even advanced HTML components. You can tell Outlook to add a signature to the end of your e-mail messages.

Creating an AutoSignature

To create an AutoSignature, choose the Tools menu's Options command and click the Mail Format tab. Then click Signature Picker. Click New in the Signature Picker dialog box to begin creating a new signature.

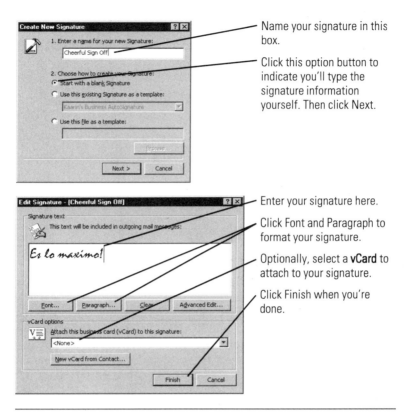

Name your signature in this box.

Click this option button to indicate you'll type the signature information yourself. Then click Next.

Enter your signature here.

Click Font and Paragraph to format your signature.

Optionally, select a **vCard** to attach to your signature.

Click Finish when you're done.

Using an AutoSignature in a Single Message

To use an AutoSignature in a message, display the Message form and click the Signature toolbar button. Then choose the signature you want from the pop-up menu. If the signature you want isn't listed on the menu, choose More and then select the signature you want to use in the Select A Signature dialog box.

continues

AutoSignature *(continued)*

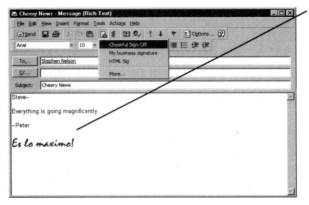

This block of text is the AutoSignature.

Using an AutoSignature in All Your Messages

To use an AutoSignature in all your messages, display the Inbox folder and choose the Tools menu's Options command. When Outlook displays the Options dialog box, click the Mail Format tab. Then select the signature you want in the Use This Signature By Default drop-down list box.

If you don't want to use a signature when replying to a message or forwarding a message, select this check box.

Signature options

The amount of signature options you have depends on the **message format** you use. For example, if you use Plain Text, you can insert ASCII art but not image files. If you use HTML, you can use Microsoft FrontPage Express to create fancy HTML signatures. Note also that a signature you create in one format may not be available to messages written in another.

Bcc SEE Blind Carbon Copy

Blind Carbon Copy

A blind carbon copy is a **copy** of a **message** sent to one **recipient** without the recipient's name appearing on the copies sent to the other recipients. For example, a blind carbon copy of an employee's annual review might be sent to the human resources manager of a company without the employee knowing. To send blind carbon copies, display the **Message form** and then choose the View menu's Bcc Field command. Use the Bcc box to name the recipients to whom you want to send a blind carbon copy of a message.

Once you choose the View menu's Bcc Field command, Outlook adds the Bcc box to the Message form.

Body SEE Message Body

Bullets

Outlook lets you include bullets in e-mail messages. To do this, select the paragraphs that you want to turn into a bulleted list and click the Bullets toolbar button. Note as well that if you create messages using HTML or Microsoft Word as your e-mail editor, you can also create numbered lists using the Numbering toolbar button.

continues

Bullets *(continued)*

The Bullets toolbar button.

Bullets work well in short lists.

Bullets are a paragraph formatting option

When you click the Bullets toolbar button, Outlook doesn't add a bullet to the beginning of each line but to the beginning of each paragraph you selected. To start each line with a bullet, you need to create short, one-line paragraphs by pressing the Enter key at the end of each line.

Busy Time

Outlook calls the time slots that you've already filled with **appointments** your *busy times.* You can see your busy times blocked out on the **Calendar.** The opposite of busy time is free time, by the way.

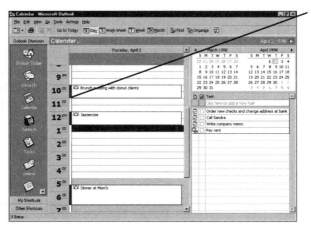

On a color monitor, the busy times appear in blue.

Calendar

The Calendar is an **Outlook folder** that lets you schedule **appointments,** meetings, or any of the ordinary activities and **events** that seem to fill up everyone's days. Your dentist appointment. The kids' birthdays. Your anniversary. You get the idea.

If you've used **Microsoft Schedule+,** the Calendar will look pretty familiar to you. (Incidentally, if you're a former Schedule+ user, you can import your old schedule into Outlook. See the entry on the **Import And Export** command.)

The Calendar folder has several components.

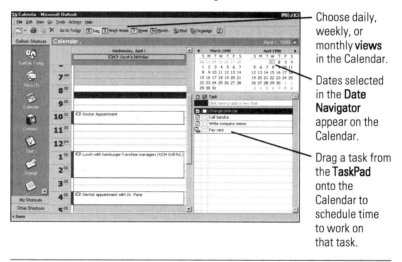

Choose daily, weekly, or monthly **views** in the Calendar.

Dates selected in the **Date Navigator** appear on the Calendar.

Drag a task from the **TaskPad** onto the Calendar to schedule time to work on that task.

Changing the Calendar View

Outlook lets you view your Calendar information in a variety of ways. Accordingly, you will probably want to experiment with the Calendar on your own to find the views that work best for you.

continues

Calendar (continued)

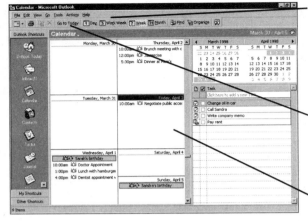

Click these toolbar buttons to view a single day, the work week, the week, or the entire month.

Click the Go To Today toolbar button to view today's schedule.

This is the Week view of the Calendar.

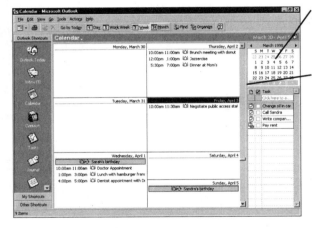

Click in the Date Navigator to move around in the Calendar.

Drag to the right the divider between the Date Navigator and the Calendar to display only one month of the Date Navigator and view more about your appointments in the Day, Week, or Month view.

Customizing the Calendar view

You can also customize the view of your Calendar. This works the same way as it does for Outlook's other folders. Just choose the View menu's Current View command and the Current View submenu's Customize Current View Command. In the View Summary dialog box, you can change the way appointments and events are filtered. You can also change the amount of information displayed in the Calendar by adding or removing **fields** from the view. And depending on the view you have displayed, you can change the way Outlook sorts and groups appointments and events in lists.

Setting Calendar Display Options

You can set various Calendar display options, including establishing the work week and designating working hours, by using the Calendar Options dialog box. To display the Calendar Options dialog box, choose the Tools menu's Options command, click the Preferences tab, and then click Calendar Options.

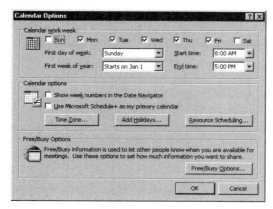

Adding Birthdays and Anniversaries to the Calendar

In Outlook, activities or occasions that last a full day or more are called events. Events include occasions such as conventions, trade shows, or birthdays. Events differ from appointments in that they don't occupy time in your schedule. To show that events occur but don't take time, Outlook records events by simply placing a notice, or banner, on the Calendar. You may want to add annual events such as birthdays and anniversaries, to your Calendar. To add an annual event such as a birthday or anniversary, follow these steps:

1 Click the Calendar icon on the Outlook Bar.

2 Choose the Actions menu's New All Day Event command. Outlook displays the Event form.

continues

Calendar *(continued)*

3 Click the Recurrence toolbar button.

4 Under Recurrence Pattern, click the Yearly option button and enter the date of the birthday or anniversary. Click OK. Outlook redisplays the Untitled—Recurring Event form.

5 In the Subject box, name the birthday or anniversary. Outlook renames the Event dialog box with the name of the event.

6 Set a **Reminder** if you need time to prepare for an event. (In the case of a birthday, for example, you might want time to send a card or buy a gift.)

7 Type any notes or comments.

8 Optionally, click Categories. Outlook displays the Categories dialog box.

9 Select a category, and then click OK.

10 Click the Save And Close toolbar button.

Adding Holidays to the Calendar

Outlook knows the names and dates of the official holidays in many of the world's countries and for several religions. To add holidays to your Calendar, follow these steps:

1 Choose the Tools menu's Options command. Outlook displays the Options dialog box.

2 Click the Preferences tab.

3 Click Calendar Options. Outlook displays the Calendar Options dialog box.

4 Click Add Holidays. Outlook displays the Add Holidays To Calendar dialog box.

5 Check the holiday set you want to add in the list box, and click OK.

6 Click OK again in the Calendar Options dialog box. Outlook adds the holidays to your Calendar.

Using the Calendar to schedule appointments and meetings

To quickly block out time for appointments or meetings, display the daily Calendar for the day on which you want to schedule the appointment or meeting. Select the block of time the appointment or meeting will occupy. Right-click the selected block of time, and an appointment or meeting command from the shortcut menu. Outlook displays the appropriate form and enters the starting and ending times for you. You just fill out the rest of the form, click the Save And Close toolbar button, and you're all done.

SEE ALSO   Plan A Meeting Wizard; Second Time Zone

Categories

You can assign Outlook **items** to various categories to make them easier to **sort, group,** and **find.** Outlook has 20 built-in categories, including business, personal, ideas, and miscellaneous. And it's easy to create new categories as you need them.

continues

Categories *(continued)*

Assigning an Item to a Category

To assign an item to a category, follow these steps:

1 Right-click the item in the information viewer.

2 Choose the shortcut menu's Categories command. Outlook displays the Categories dialog box.

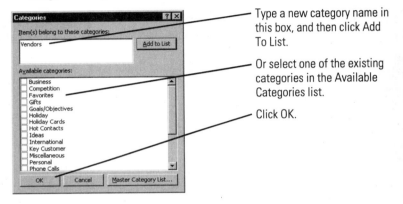

Type a new category name in this box, and then click Add To List.

Or select one of the existing categories in the Available Categories list.

Click OK.

Using categories to group tasks into projects

Outlook doesn't automatically group tasks into projects the way Microsoft Schedule+ does, but that needn't stop you from using Outlook for basic project management. Just create a category for each project you start. For example, you could create a category called "Renovating the bathroom" or "Fall marketing campaign." Thereafter, every time you add a new task associated with the bathroom renovation project or the marketing campaign, you assign it to one of the new categories. Then you can group tasks by category to collect all the project tasks under the same heading.

Cc SEE Copy

Character Formatting

You can format characters in **messages**. Probably the easiest way to do it is by using the Formatting **toolbar** along the top of the **Message form**. The following figure points out the location of the Formatting toolbar. To format a bit of text, select the text and then click a Formatting toolbar button or select an entry in a Formatting toolbar drop-down list box. Before you add character formatting to messages, however, keep in mind that depending on the e-mail client the message recipient has, he or she may not be able to see the formatting you apply. So don't rely on formatting to carry your message's message.

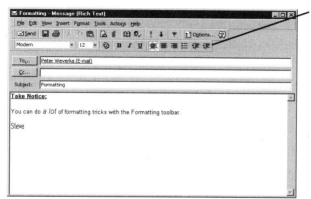

This is the Formatting toolbar.

Confused about which toolbar button is which?

When you move the mouse pointer over a toolbar button, Outlook displays a small pop-up box with the tool's name. If you forget which tool is which, you can use these pop-up boxes, called ToolTips, to jog your memory.

SEE ALSO   Alignment

Check Names

You can verify that you typed the names of message **recipients** correctly. To do this, click the Check Names toolbar button in the **Message form** window.

continues

Check Names *(continued)*

You don't have to type someone's entire name when you address an e-mail message, however—only enough of the name for Outlook to identify the recipient. When Kaarin sends a message addressed to "Stephen N" on our little **network,** for example, it gets to me even though the **Global Address List** shows my name as "Stephen Nelson." And I can send a message back to "Kaarin" or even just "Kaa" even though the Global Address List shows her name as "Kaarin Dolliver." When you click Check Names, Outlook replaces the partial name you entered with the full user name—provided it can match the partial name to a name on the Global Address List. (If Outlook can't figure out to whom you want to send a message, it asks you for more information about the recipient.)

SEE ALSO Spelling Checker

Client

Local area networks (LANs) consist of two parts: clients and **servers.** If you're using Outlook as part of a LAN, the client part of the system (Outlook) runs on your computer; the server part (Microsoft **Exchange Server**), not surprisingly, runs on the server. The client part can function happily in just about any new version of Windows, including Windows 95, Windows 98, and Windows NT. So this book assumes you're running Outlook on top of Windows. But Microsoft also sells versions of Outlook and its cousin Exchange that work on other computers and on top of other operating systems.

SEE ALSO Outlook Client

Columns

If you look closely at the right side of the Outlook window, you'll notice that it often provides several pieces of information about the items listed, depending upon the particular **Outlook folder** that's open. When the **Inbox** list is displayed, for example, icons identify messages that the **sender** flagged as important or that include an **attachment.** And the **information viewer** also identifies who sent the message and what its **subject** is.

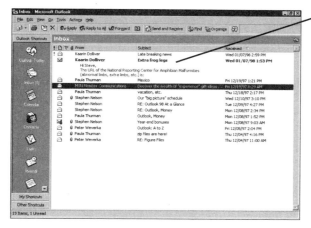

The Inbox information viewer provides several columns of information about messages.

Editing View Columns

You can decide for yourself which information the Inbox displays in its information viewer. To do so, follow these steps:

1 Choose the View menu's Current View command.

2 Choose the Current View submenu's Customize Current View command. Outlook displays the View Summary dialog box.

3 Click Fields.

4 Use the boxes and buttons in the Show Fields dialog box to add and remove message information.

To add a **field,** click an entry in the Available Fields list box and then click Add.

To remove a field, click an entry in the Show These Fields In This Order list box and then click Remove.

To change the position of a column, click it and then click Move Up or Move Down.

Different folders use different fields

The available fields in the Show Fields dialog box differ from one Outlook folder to another. In the **Calendar** folder, for example, available fields include Created, End, and Start. And in the Contacts folder, they include Job Title, Company, and Business Phone. You can change which fields you have available by selecting a different entry in the Select Available Fields From drop-down list box.

Connection Wizard

Microsoft Internet Explorer comes with a Connection Wizard that you can use to set up a new Dial-Up Networking connection even after you initially set up Outlook and Internet Explorer. To use the Connection Wizard, click the Start button and then choose Programs, Internet Explorer, and Connection Wizard. By following the on-screen instructions, the wizard does everything necessary to connect your computer to the Internet. Once you run the wizard, you should be able to browse the **World Wide Web,** send and receive **e-mail,** and view newsgroups.

SEE ALSO   Newsreader

Contacts List   SEE   Contacts

Contacts

The Contacts folder provides you with an electronic phone and address book for tracking nearly every conceivable kind of information about your friends, family, and associates.

You enter contact information in the New Contact **form.** If your contacts are from large companies (or if they're just especially hip individuals), you can even include their **Web page** addresses.

Like the other **Outlook folders,** Contacts can be viewed in several different ways. Address Cards is a particularly useful **view**—it's like an electronic Rolodex file with a built-in index.

Adding a Contact to the Contacts List

To add a new contact to the Contacts list, either click the New Contact toolbar button or choose the File menu's New command and the New submenu's Contact command. Outlook displays the Untitled—Contact form.

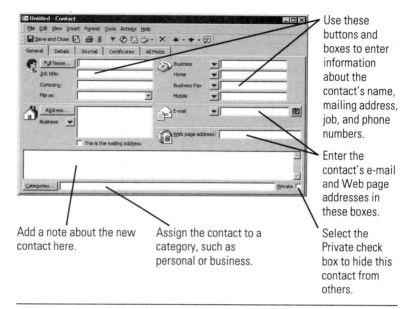

Use these buttons and boxes to enter information about the contact's name, mailing address, job, and phone numbers.

Enter the contact's e-mail and Web page addresses in these boxes.

Add a note about the new contact here.

Assign the contact to a category, such as personal or business.

Select the Private check box to hide this contact from others.

Changing the View of the Contacts List

To change the view of the Contacts list, first display it by clicking the Contacts icon on the Outlook Bar. Choose the View menu's Current View command, and then choose one of the Current View submenu's commands.

Choose the Customize Current View command (which appears on the Current View submenu) to add or rearrange the fields in the current view or to change the way Outlook groups, sorts, and filters contacts in the current view. Choose the Define Views command (which also appears on the Current View submenu) to add a view of your own design to the View list.

continues

Contacts *(continued)*

Another way to change the current view

If you click the Contact toolbar's Organize button, Outlook gives you another way to change the view: click the Using Views hyperlink, and then select a view in the list box that Outlook supplies.

Looking Up a Contact in Address Cards View

Looking up a contact in Address Cards view is just like using a rotary file. You just spin the file, electronically, of course, until you find the card you want. To display your contacts in Address Cards view, choose the View menu's Current View command and the Current View submenu's Address Cards command.

Address Cards view displays contacts as a list of Rolodex-like cards.

Click the index letter corresponding to the name of the contact you want to look up.

Double-click the name of the contact to display the Contact form.

Conversation Thread

A conversation thread is a **message** and all its **replies.** For example, if I send you an e-mail message that asks about a round of golf next Friday and you e-mail me a message saying that Friday doesn't work but Saturday sounds mighty fine, our two messages constitute a conversation thread.

Sometimes it's helpful to view the messages in a mail **folder** by conversation thread, so Outlook supplies a view called By Conversation Topic that lets you do that. To use this view, simply choose the View menu's Current View command and the Current View submenu's By Conversation Topic command. To view the messages in a conversation thread, click the plus sign next to the conversation.

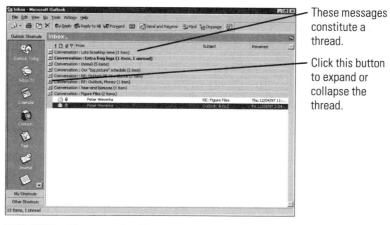

These messages constitute a thread.

Click this button to expand or collapse the thread.

SEE ALSO   Newsreader; Views

Copy

You can send someone a copy of a **message** that you're sending to someone else. All you need to do is enter the person's **e-mail name** in the Cc box. Or if you don't know the person's e-mail name, click Cc. When Outlook displays the Select Names dialog box (which shows the contents of your **Address Book** lists), use it to identify the person to whom you want to send the copy.

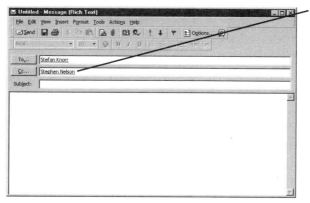

Enter the e-mail name of the person you want to receive the copy here.

SEE ALSO   Blind Carbon Copy

Custom Form

Outlook allows you to use custom forms to collect information from lots of different places. **Forms** sound funny at first, but they are actually very useful. You (or somebody else in your **organization**) might create an expense report form so that employees can describe and submit payment requests for reimbursable expenses. Or you might create a project status form so that the people working together can either report on or see how the project is progressing. You can create forms for all Outlook items (including **posts**) except Notes. You might even create a form that lets you share other, more entertaining information.

Date Navigator

The Date Navigator is the small monthly calendar that appears in the upper right corner of the **Calendar** folder. You use the Date Navigator to pick the date or dates whose schedules are displayed in the Calendar.

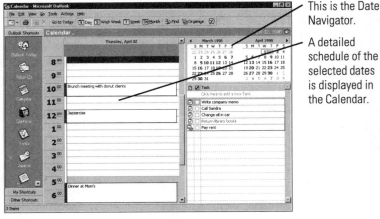

This is the Date Navigator.

A detailed schedule of the selected dates is displayed in the Calendar.

Today's date appears in a red square.

Days with scheduled activities appear in boldface.

Using the Date Navigator to Display Different Days' Schedules on the Calendar

Click a date to display that day's schedule in the Calendar. Drag the pointer over a series of dates to select them all, or select nonadjacent dates by holding down the Ctrl key and clicking each date.

Moving from One Month to Another in Date Navigator

Click the left arrow to display the previous month; click the right arrow to display the next month. Click the month name in the Date Navigator's title bar, and a list of month names appears. Move the pointer over one of the month names and release the mouse button to display that month in the Date Navigator.

Rescheduling an Appointment Using the Date Navigator

Simply drag a scheduled appointment from the Calendar to a date in the Date Navigator to reschedule an appointment for a different day.

SEE ALSO   Appointment

Deferred Delivery

You can tell Outlook to defer delivery of a message. In other words, you can say, "Okay, deliver this message, but not before some point in the future." To defer delivery of a message, display the message in a **Message form** and click the Options toolbar button. When Outlook displays the Message Options dialog box, select the Do Not Deliver Before check box and specify the deferral date.

Enter the deferral date here.

Defining Views SEE Views

Delegate Access

When you're using Outlook as a Microsoft **Exchange Server** client, you can give other users on your network delegate access permissions. Delegate access permissions specify who can do what with your Personal Folders. For example, you can give other people on your network permission to view your **Calendar** and make or cancel appointments for you. Or you can give people permission to send and receive e-mail messages on your behalf. To add a delegate, choose the Tools menu's Options command, click the Delegates tab, and then click Add. Use the Add Users dialog box to select the name of the person to whom you want to give delegate access permissions. Then use the Delegate Permissions dialog box for that user to specify the permission level you want to give the delegate for each of your Personal Folders. Before you start fooling around with these settings, however, you might just want to check with your network **administrator** to see whether your company has policies regarding the delegate access feature and access permissions in general. It probably does.

Delivery Receipt

The United States Postal Service, as you might know, offers a special service called registered mail. With registered mail, you get a delivery receipt, signed by the recipient, to prove that your letter or package truly reached its destination. Microsoft **Exchange Server** provides a similar service with its delivery receipts. You can ask the Exchange server to confirm that a **message** was delivered. To do this, click the Options toolbar button.

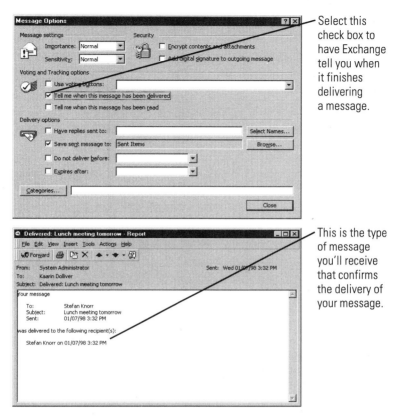

Select this check box to have Exchange tell you when it finishes delivering a message.

This is the type of message you'll receive that confirms the delivery of your message.

SEE ALSO   Read Receipt

Digital ID

Have you ever seen one of those sealing wax kits? Nowadays, I think mostly kids use them. But a long time ago, the kings and queens of Europe used them to seal their messages. They dripped hot wax over the envelope flap and then made an impression in the soft wax with their signet rings. When recipients received the letters, they could tell right away that they came from, for example, the Holy Roman Emperor. All they had to do was look at the impression made by the ring. What's more, they could tell whether the letter had been tampered with by seeing if the wax was still in place.

continues

Digital ID *(continued)*

Digital IDs, or certificates, work in a similar manner. They sign and sometimes seal a **message** so that its **recipient** can tell who really sent the message and be certain that no one tampered with the message en route.

Using a Digital ID

To use a digital ID, you first sign up with a digital ID verification service. Microsoft Corporation recommends you use the VeriSign service. You can sign up for the VeriSign service by visiting the VeriSign Web site at www.verisign.com and then following the site's on-screen instructions. (At this writing, you'll pay around $10 a year for the digital ID.)

After you sign up with the verification service and install the digital ID (following the verification service's instructions), you can send digitally signed messages to recipients. You can also encrypt messages to certain recipients.

To add a digital signature to a message, click the Options toolbar button and select the Add Digital Signature To Outgoing Message check box before you send the message. To seal a message with encryption, select the Encrypt Message Contents And Attachments check box. Click Close to close the Message Options dialog box, and then send the message in the usual way.

When you send a recipient a sealed or signed message, Outlook attaches a certificate to your message. The first time someone receives a certificate attachment, he or she needs to save the certificate. You save certificate attachments in the same way that you save other attachments. For example, you can right-click the attachment to display the shortcut menu and then choose the Save As command.

Verifying a Digital Signature

Usually, when you open a digitally signed message, the certificate automatically appears so that you can immediately verify that the message hasn't been tampered with. If the certificate doesn't automatically open, choose the File menu's Properties command and click the Security tab.

This mesage doesn't pass the test because it was sent from a different address and might have been forged.

SEE ALSO   Encryption; Security

Discussions SEE Post

Distribution List

Using Outlook's **Address Book,** you can create a distribution list of people to whom you want to send a **message.** That sounds like no big deal, but distribution lists—the Internet Only version of Outlook calls them *groups*—are actually pretty neat because they make it easy to send a message to a lot of people. Rather than separately listing the name of each **recipient** to whom you want to send a message, you just specify the distribution list.

Creating a Distribution List

As long as you've already added the recipients to your **Personal Address Book** or **Contacts** folder, or you can find the recipients in the **Global Address List,** it's easy to create a long distribution list. To create the list, follow the steps on the next page:

continues

D

Distribution List *(continued)*

1 Display the Address Book by clicking the Address Book toolbar button or choosing the Tools menu's Address Book command. Outlook displays the Address Book dialog box.

2 Click the New toolbar button. Outlook displays the New Entry dialog box.

Select Personal Distribution List in the list box.

Specify where you want Outlook to store the distribution list in the In The drop-down list box. Then click OK.

3 Name the personal distribution list by entering a brief description in the Name box.

4 Click Add/Remove Members. Outlook displays a dialog box that allows you to choose names from your Address Book lists.

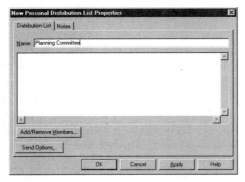

5 Double-click the **e-mail names** of the people you want to add to the personal distribution list.

6 Click OK when you finish building the distribution list.

The New Group toolbar button

If you installed the Internet Only version of Outlook, the procedure for creating a distribution list is a little different. To create a distribution list, open your Address Book and click the New Group toolbar button. Enter a name for the group in the Group Name box, and then click Select Members. Use the Select Group Members dialog box to add members to the group.

Using a Distribution List

To send the same e-mail message to everyone named on a distribution list, just enter the distribution list name in the To box of the **Message form.**

Domain

Domain is both a Windows NT term and an Internet term. Unfortunately, however, the term means slightly different things in each case. In Windows NT, a domain is a collection of **servers** and **clients** that get administered together. A Windows NT **network** can have a single domain (usually the case with small networks), or it can have several different domains (usually the case with big or geographically dispersed networks).

An Internet domain is different. From our perspective as users, a domain is just a name that identifies a network to the Internet and to Internet users. (It's for this reason, by the way, that people's e-mail addresses include an Internet domain name.)

This all sounds terribly confusing, but maybe a quick example will clear things up. Take the case of Microsoft Corporation. Microsoft uses many different Windows NT domains for its internal computer network, but it uses only one Internet domain, microsoft.com.

SEE ALSO Organization

Drafts

By default, Outlook automatically saves messages you're writing to your Drafts folder every three minutes. And if you close a **message** without sending it, Outlook asks whether you want to save the message. If you indicate you do, Outlook keeps a copy of the partially completed message in your Drafts folder. To view the contents of the Drafts folder, click My Shortcuts on the **Outlook Bar** and then click the Drafts icon. To open a message that is stored in the Drafts folder, double-click it. To complete and send a message you've opened, make your changes and click the Send toolbar button.

Electronic Mail SEE E-Mail

E

E-Mail

E-mail is an abbreviation that stands for electronic mail. The term describes the **messages** that people send from one computer to another. In most cases, e-mail is transmitted instantaneously—or almost instantaneously. You send a message, and a few seconds or minutes later, someone receives it.

E-Mail Alias

An e-mail alias is usually the same as an **e-mail name.** It's the name you use to send someone an e-mail message.

E-Mail Etiquette

Good manners are never complicated, so you won't be surprised to learn that there's nothing particularly tricky about the etiquette of e-mail. Be courteous. Never say something you don't want repeated (or forwarded). Don't waste your recipient's time by sending useless messages or replies. In short, treat people as you yourself want to be treated, and respect their time.

E-Mail Filters SEE Inbox Filters

E-Mail Name

If you want to send me an e-mail **message,** you can't just type "Stephen L. Nelson" in the To box. My name might mean a lot to me, but to Outlook and the Internet, my name means hardly anything. What Outlook and the Internet use to uniquely identify me is my e-mail name. Stphnlnlsn, my e-mail name on The Microsoft Network, does mean something. And if you sent an e-mail message to the Internet address stphnlnlsn@msn.com, it would actually get to me. I might even read it. (I'm joking. Of course I'd read it.)

Encryption

When you encrypt something—like an e-mail **message**—you scramble the information so that it can't be read by anyone who doesn't know how to unscramble it. When the **recipient** gets your e-mail message, he or she decrypts, or unscrambles, it in order to read it. To encrypt messages, you need a **digital ID.** For someone on the Internet to read a message you've encrypted, you need to have first sent them a digital ID certificate.

Eudora

Eudora is an e-mail client, just as Outlook is. This bit of information isn't all that relevant to this Field Guide—since it's about Outlook. But if you used to work with Eudora, you'll be interested to know that Outlook can probably grab both e-mail messages and e-mail names and addresses from Eudora so that you can use them in Outlook. Outlook does this, by the way, as you install it. One more thing: did you know that Eudora was named after the writer Eudora Welty?

Event

In Outlook an event is a notation in the **Calendar** that doesn't occupy a time slot. This sounds funny, but take the example of a child's birthday. You might want to note this event on your Calendar—so you remember to buy a gift, say—even though the event doesn't actually take time out of your work day. To put it another way, events are occasions that you want to remember but not necessarily schedule time for.

Creating an Event

To add an event to your Calendar, click the Calendar icon on the Outlook Bar. Choose the Actions menu's New All Day Event command. Then use the Event dialog box to describe the event and its timing.

continues

Event *(continued)*

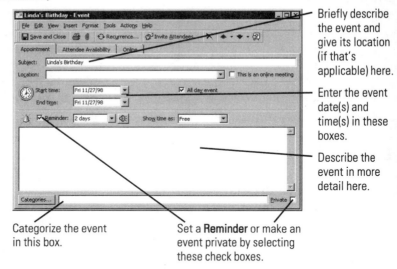

Briefly describe the event and give its location (if that's applicable) here.

Enter the event date(s) and time(s) in these boxes.

Describe the event in more detail here.

Categorize the event in this box.

Set a **Reminder** or make an event private by selecting these check boxes.

Viewing Event Information

You can view event information in several ways. Outlook doesn't block out time on your Calendar for events. Events appear on the Calendar as notices above the day or days they are scheduled. You can also choose the View menu's Current View command and then choose the Current View submenu's Events command.

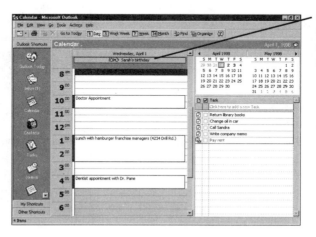

On the daily Calendar, all-day events show up here.

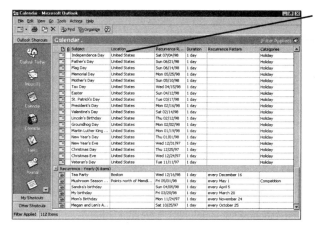

When you choose the Events view, all your scheduled events show up in a list.

Exchange Server

Microsoft Exchange Server is software that runs on a network server. With Exchange and Outlook, you and the people you work with can pass messages around your network. Exchange also lets you coordinate people's schedules—figuring out, for example, when people next have time in their **Calendars** for a meeting.

SEE ALSO   **Plan A Meeting Wizard**

Favorites Folder

The Favorites folder, a subfolder in the Windows folder, is a place where you can store files, shortcuts, or even other folders that you use frequently, so you know where to find them. In addition, your Internet browser stores your favorite **URLs** in the Favorites folder. To view the contents of your Favorites folder using Outlook, click Other Shortcuts on the Outlook Bar and then click the Favorites icon.

continues

Favorites Folder *(continued)*

If your Favorites folder has subfolders, they show up on the Favorites list, too.

Field Chooser SEE Fields

Fields

Outlook provides a variety of fields to describe details of particular **items.** You can add and remove fields from **views** of Outlook items. You can also create entirely new fields of your own.

In views that list items in a table format, such as the Messages view of the **Inbox,** fields are the **columns** of the table. In other types of views (such as the Address Cards view of the **Contacts** list), fields can appear as rows.

Changing the Fields in a View

To change the fields displayed in a view, choose the View menu's Current View command and then choose the Current View submenu's Customize Current View command. When Outlook displays the View Summary dialog box, click Fields. Outlook displays the Show Fields dialog box.

Click this button to add fields to the view.

Click this button to remove fields from the view.

Click these buttons to rearrange the order of fields in the view.

Click this button to display the New Field dialog box and create a new field.

Display this box's drop-down list to show other available fields.

SEE ALSO   Group By Box; Views

File

A file is what you (and the computer **programs** you use) store on your computer's hard disk. As important as your departmental budget may be to you, to your computer it's just another file—the same as any other. That novel you've been slaving away on for the last 11 years? Another file. You get the picture.

As far as Outlook goes, you need to know two things about files: you can attach files to Outlook items (including the **messages** you send), and you can make it easier to share files on a network by copying the files into **Public Folders.**

SEE ALSO   Post

File Extension

In Windows, a three-letter file extension at the end of a filename identifies the file type. You typically don't have to worry about file extensions, by the way. The file extension is really just for Windows. But you sometimes see file extensions, and by glancing at them you can tell what type of file you are looking at.

The three-letter string following the period is the file extension.

Filters

Filters allow you to choose the items you want to display in the **information viewer**. Filters narrow down the list of items in a folder to just the ones that meet the criteria you set. To filter items, choose the View menu's Current View command and then the Current View submenu's Customize Current View command. When Outlook displays the View Summary dialog box, click Filter to display the Filter dialog box.

Use the More Choices and Advanced tabs to establish additional search criteria.

Use these buttons and boxes to find the items that meet your criteria.

Click this button to remove all filters and display the entire contents of the selected folder.

Outlook reminds you that you've filtered the information viewer by adding the words *Filter Applied* to the folder title bar.

SEE ALSO   Inbox Filters; Task Filters; Views

Find

If you work in a large **organization** where everybody uses e-mail, if you maintain a long Contacts list, or if you're a manager who's constantly assigning tasks and attending meetings, the volume of items you need to track can be staggering. In such an environment, it's easy to lose or misplace items of importance. Fortunately, Outlook provides a powerful Find tool you can use in two ways to locate lost messages, tasks, contacts, and other items.

Finding Items

If you're pretty sure you know in which folder the item you're looking for is located, you can conduct a simple search for the item by displaying the item's folder and clicking the Find toolbar button to display the Find pane.

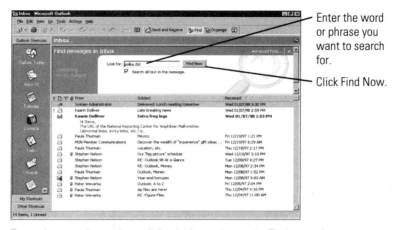

Enter the word or phrase you want to search for.

Click Find Now.

To conduct an advanced search for the item, choose the Tools menu's Advanced Find command and then use the Advanced Find dialog box.

Enter the text you want to search for.

Click Browse to select the folders you want Outlook to search for the item.

Click Find Now to begin your search.

Use the buttons and boxes to describe more details about the item you want to find.

Tell Outlook what part of the item contains the text you entered.

About the More Choices and Advanced tabs

You can specify additional search criteria on the More Choices and Advanced tabs. The More Choices tab lets you tell Outlook to look for items of a certain size or items that are assigned to a certain category. The Advanced tab allows you to add even more specific criteria.

continues

Find *(continued)*

Finding Outlook Items Using the Start Menu

When you installed Outlook, Windows added a new command to the Find submenu on your Start menu: Using Microsoft Outlook. When you choose this command, Windows displays the Find dialog box so that you can search for Outlook items from anywhere in your computer without having to launch Outlook. You can also use the Find Submenu's On The Internet command to conduct an Internet search using a search service. Or you can choose the People command to find lost friends on the Internet using a directory service.

Flame

A flame is an **e-mail message** that's mean and nasty. If you e-mail a message to me that says I'm a complete moron who is utterly incapable of constructing a sentence, for example, that's a flame. By the way, if I e-mail you back a message that says your mother wears army boots and your sister is ugly, we have what is known as a "flame war."

Flames, as you might guess, violate all the rules of e-mail good manners and etiquette. But because some people have the maturity of grade-schoolers, you see quite a few flames—particularly on the **Internet.** On a philosophical note, I suspect that the anonymity of e-mail and the Internet has something to do with this meanness. People are more apt to say mean and threatening things when they don't have to see the other person's face or worry about running into the other person at the grocery store or a staff meeting.

Folder

Outlook uses folders to organize Outlook items. The Inbox and Outbox folders store message items you've received or plan to send. The Contacts folder stores contact items. The Tasks folder stores task items, and so on.

By the way, it's easy to create new folders. Select the folder or mailbox in which you want to place a new folder. Then choose the File menu's New command and the File submenu's Folder command.

Name the new folder.

Specify where it should be located.

Click OK.

SEE ALSO   Folder Banner; Folder List; Outlook Folders; Subfolder

Folder Banner

The Folder Banner is the bar below the toolbars in the Outlook window. On the left side of the Folder Banner, Outlook displays the name of the selected folder. You can click the folder name to display a list of all the **Outlook folders.** The Folder Banner also displays the selected folder's icon and additional information such as today's date in the **Calendar** or the alphabetical range of contacts displayed in the **Contacts** folder.

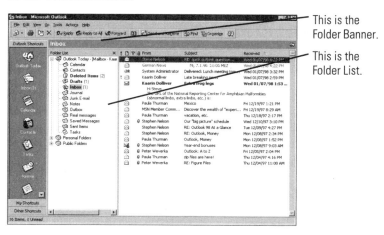

This is the Folder Banner.

This is the Folder List.

Folder List

The term *Folder List* refers to the folder tree, or hierarchy, that Outlook displays in the left portion of the Outlook window. If you've worked with Outlook for more than a day or two, you already know that Outlook uses these **folders** to organize various **items.** Unlike the Outlook Bar, which you can customize to list only certain Outlook folders, the Folder List lists all of your Outlook folders. In addition, you can use Outlook just like you'd use Windows Explorer or My Computer—to display the folder hierarchy of your entire computer and network. If the Folder List doesn't appear in the Outlook program window and you want to see it, click the folder name on the **Folder Banner.**

SEE ALSO   Outlook Folders

Folder View

A Folder view is a certain way to look at the information in a specific **folder.** For example, you can organize the **messages** in the **Inbox** folder by specifying which **columns** (or **fields**) appear, how messages are grouped or sorted, and whether any e-mail **filters** are used. Outlook offers a variety of predefined Folder **views.**

Creating a Folder View

To create a Folder view, choose the View menu's Current View command and then the Current View submenu's Define Views command. When Outlook displays the Define Views dialog box, click New. Outlook displays the Create A New View dialog box.

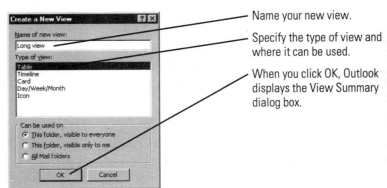

Name your new view.

Specify the type of view and where it can be used.

When you click OK, Outlook displays the View Summary dialog box.

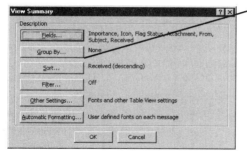

Click these buttons to specify the columns of message information (fields), grouping, sorting, filtering, and formatting you want. Then click OK.

Using a Folder View

To see and select a predefined view, choose the View menu's Current View command and then choose one of the Current View submenu's commands.

SEE ALSO   Fields; Grouping Items; Sorting

Font

If you've worked with a word processor—say, **Microsoft Word**—you probably know that a font is simply a typeface that looks a certain way. What you may not know is that because Outlook happily passes back and forth what are called Rich Text Format (RTF) files, it lets you include all sorts of fonts in messages.

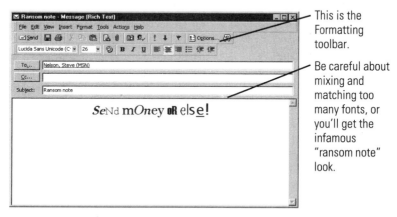

This is the Formatting toolbar.

Be careful about mixing and matching too many fonts, or you'll get the infamous "ransom note" look.

continues

Font *(continued)*

It's easy to format a **message**. With the **Message form** displayed, select the text and then click the Formatting toolbar's buttons and activate the drop-down list boxes to make your changes. You can use the Font box to change the current text selection's font, for example. And you can use the Font Size box to specify the font point size. You can also use the Format menu's Font command to make changes to a font. When you choose this command, Outlook displays the Font dialog box. You can use it to make your formatting changes.

Select a font.

Choose a font style.

Specify a point size.

Watch the Sample box to see the effect of your formatting choices.

Form

In Outlook, you use forms to collect and view information. For example, when you create a **message,** you use a form called, cleverly enough, the **Message form.** In this form you name the **recipient,** enter the message **subject,** and type in the **message body.** Outlook comes with predefined forms for writing and reading **e-mail** messages, of course. But you can create specialized forms for collecting and viewing other types of information, too: employee expense reports, project schedule updates, and so on.

SEE ALSO   Custom Form

Form Design

You can create your own customized **forms** by choosing the Tools menu's Forms command and the Forms submenu's Design A Form command. This book doesn't cover form design in any detail because, alas, there isn't enough space.

SEE ALSO   Custom Form

Forward

You can send a copy of a **message** you receive to someone else. To do this, select or display the message and then click the Forward toolbar button. Outlook opens a **form** that you use to create your response.

Free Time SEE Busy Time

Global Address List

If you work on a network that includes an **Exchange server,** the Global Address List lists all the people in your **organization** to whom you can send e-mail. The Global Address List can be viewed by clicking the Address Book toolbar button and then selecting Global Address List from the Show Names From The drop-down list box.

If your organization is huge, with hundreds or thousands of users, the Global Address List isn't a useful way to find the e-mail names of people you correspond with regularly. Instead, add your regular correspondents' e-mail names to your Contacts folder or to a **Personal Address Book.**

Group By Box

If you've chosen to display the Advanced toolbar—you can do this by choosing the View menu's Toolbars command and then by choosing Advanced—you can group and ungroup **messages** and **tasks** in the Group By box. To use the Group By box, click the Group By Box toolbar button. Outlook opens a space—the Group By box—between the **Folder Banner** and the column headings of the **information viewer.** You can drag column headings, which are actually buttons, in and out of the Group By box to group items by those headings. Outlook groups items based on the order in which the headings appear in the box. If you don't like the order, simply rearrange the headings. And when you want to ungroup items, just drag the headings back into the information viewer.

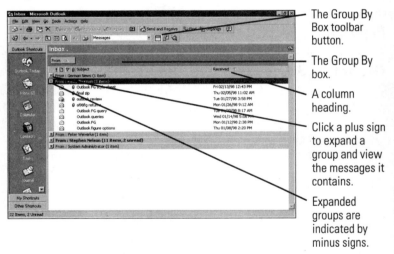

The Group By Box toolbar button.

The Group By box.

A column heading.

Click a plus sign to expand a group and view the messages it contains.

Expanded groups are indicated by minus signs.

SEE ALSO Grouping Items; Views

Grouping Items

You can tell Outlook to group **items** with similar characteristics. For example, you can tell Outlook to group **messages** with the same **sender,** the same **subject,** and so on. To do this, choose the View menu's Current View command and then choose the Current View submenu's Customize Current View command. When Outlook displays the View Summary dialog box, click Group By. Outlook displays the Group By dialog box, which you can use to specify how you want to group items such as messages.

Specify how you want items grouped by using the Group Items By drop-down list box.

You can group items within a group by using the Then By list boxes.

SEE ALSO   Group By Box

Group Scheduling

If you work on a network that includes an **Exchange server,** you can use Outlook to schedule meetings for groups of people as long as everybody uses Outlook's **Calendar** or Microsoft Schedule+ to keep their appointment calendars. To perform such group scheduling, you use the **Plan A Meeting Wizard.**

Help

Outlook's online Help feature gives you information with just a mouse click or a keystroke. You can access the conventional Help system by choosing the Help menu's Contents And Index command. If you performed the full installation of Outlook, you also have another source of help, the **Office Assistant,** Microsoft Office's animated Help feature. If you click the Office Assistant toolbar button or choose the Help menu's Microsoft Outlook Help command, Outlook starts the Office Assistant.

HTML

The acronym HTML stands for *hypertext markup language*. HTML is what you use to create **World Wide Web** documents. In fact, for this reason, the HTML acronym is often used as the last part of a World Wide Web document name—to identify what it is. (On PCs, World Wide Web documents use the **file extension** .htm for the same reason.) Do you need to know this? No, not really. But it turns out that Outlook lets you use HTML to format e-mail messages you send, and it happily reads HTML-**formatted e-mail** you receive.

SEE ALSO Font; HTML Stationery

HTML-Formatted E-Mail

Outlook 98 accepts e-mail messages that use **HTML**. What this means is that if someone includes HTML in an e-mail message or attaches a Web page, Outlook displays whatever the HTML tells it to display.

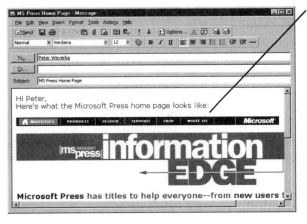

This e-mail includes HTML formatting.

SEE ALSO Address Book; HTML Stationery

HTML Stationery

Outlook comes with a variety of HTML stationery—stationery that uses fancy HTML formatting to make e-mail messages more colorful and interesting. To use HTML stationery, display the Inbox folder, choose the Actions menu's New Mail Message Using command, and then select a stationery or choose More Stationery from the submenu. When Outlook displays the Select A Stationery dialog box, double-click the HTML stationery you want to use.

SEE ALSO   **Address Book; HTML-Formatted E-Mail**

Hyperlink

You can put a link to a **World Wide Web** page or FTP site—a hyperlink—in your messages. You just need to know the **URL,** or hyperlink address, of the **Web page** or FTP site to which you want to link. To insert a hyperlink in a message, type the hyperlink address in the message area of the **Message form.** When you press the Enter key, the hyperlink becomes active.

continues

Hyperlink *(continued)*

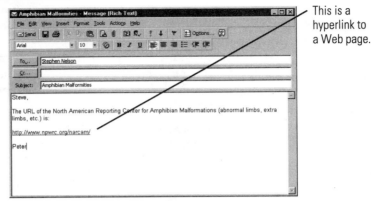

This is a hyperlink to a Web page.

If you've been using your **Web browser** to collect favorite Web pages in your **Favorites folder,** you can take advantage of the URL addresses stored in your Favorites folder to insert a shortcut to a Web page in your messages. Just click in the message area of the Message form. Then choose the Insert menu's File command. In the Insert File dialog box, click the Look In Favorites toolbar button. Make sure that Attachment is selected under Insert As (on the right side of the dialog box). Double-click the URL you want to insert in your message.

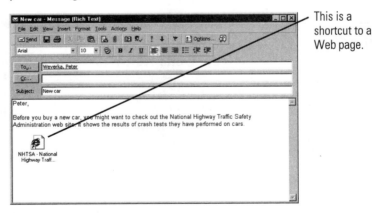

This is a shortcut to a Web page.

SEE ALSO Internet

Importance

Some of the **messages** you send are very important either to you or the **recipient.** And some of the messages aren't important at all. To deal with differences in urgency and importance, you can assign a priority, or level of importance, to the messages you write. Unless you tell it otherwise, Outlook assumes your message is of normal importance. To assign high importance to a message, click the Importance: High toolbar button. To assign low importance, click the (you guessed it) Importance: Low toolbar button. You can also assign importance and indicate a message's sensitivity by clicking the Options toolbar button when the Message form is displayed.

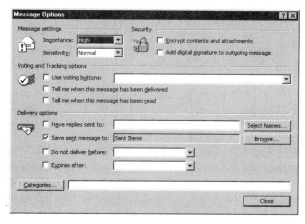

Messages' importance level and sensitivity show up in the recipient's **information viewer,** which helps the recipient identify urgent and important messages. By the way, Microsoft **Exchange Server** can be set up to deliver high-priority messages faster.

continues

Importance *(continued)*

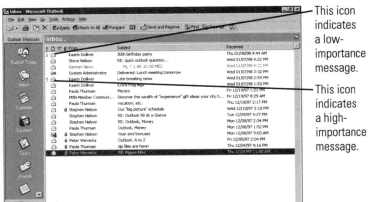

This icon indicates a low-importance message.

This icon indicates a high-importance message.

Import and Export

Outlook provides the Import And Export Wizard to help you import items and files from other applications into Outlook and export items and files from Outlook to other applications. For example, if you have a file in another personal information manager that contains names and addresses of business contacts, you can use the Import And Export Wizard to move that information into Outlook. If you're moving to Outlook from **Microsoft Schedule+**, you can import Schedule+ files into Outlook.

Importing Contacts, Appointments, and Tasks from Schedule+

To import a file from Schedule+, follow these steps:

1 Choose the File menu's Import And Export command. Outlook displays the Import And Export Wizard dialog box.

2 Select Import From Another Program Or File in the Choose An Action To Perform list box. Then click Next. Outlook displays the Import A File dialog box.

3 Select Schedule+ 7.0 in the Select File Type To Import From list box. Click Next, and Outlook displays the next Import A File dialog box.

4 If Outlook does not find the correct Schedule+ file, click Browse to locate the Schedule+ file you want to import. It will have the file extension .SCD. Click Next.

5 In the final Import A File dialog box, check to make sure that Outlook will import the items you want. Click Finish.

SEE ALSO   Calendar; Contacts

Inbox

The Inbox is the **Outlook folder** that receives and holds incoming **messages.** To view your Inbox, click the Inbox icon on the **Outlook Bar** or the Inbox folder icon in the **Folder List.**

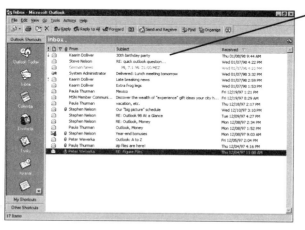

The Inbox folder lists all the messages people have sent to you.

Inbox Assistant

Microsoft Exchange, a predecessor to Outlook, provided a tool called the Inbox Assistant. The Inbox Assistant isn't part of Outlook, but you can use the **Rules Wizard** to perform all the same functions that you once relied upon the Inbox Assistant to perform.

SEE ALSO   Out Of Office Assistant

Inbox Filters

You can filter, or hide, **messages** that appear in the **information viewer** so that only messages with specific characteristics appear. For example, you can filter the information viewer so that only messages from particular (or even peculiar) **senders** get listed. Or you can filter messages so that only those marked as important or those with **attachments** get listed.

To filter messages, select the **folder** with the messages you want to filter, choose the View menu's Current View command, and then choose the Current View submenu's Customize Current View command. When Outlook displays the View Summary dialog box, click Filter. Outlook displays the Filter dialog box, which you use to describe how you want to filter messages.

Filtering Messages by Sender

To filter messages by sender, first use the From box to specify the name of the sender whose messages you want to see. If you don't know the sender's **e-mail name,** click From to display the **Address Book** and use it to identify the sender. You can, by the way, specify more than one sender—all you need to do is separate their e-mail names with semicolons.

Filtering Messages by Recipient

You can filter messages by **recipient,** too, although you wouldn't do this with the messages in your Inbox folder. (In your **Inbox,** you are the recipient.) To filter messages by recipient, use the Sent To box to specify the name of the recipient whose messages you want to see. If you don't know the recipient's e-mail name, click Sent To to display the Address Book and use it to identify the recipient. If you specify more than one recipient, separate their e-mail names with semicolons.

Select the Where I Am check box, and select The Only Person On The To Line from the drop-down list box to see only those messages that name you specifically as the recipient (rather than name a **distribution list** on which your name appears). Or select On The Cc Line With Other People to see only those messages that are actually copies of messages sent to another recipient.

Filtering Messages by Subject and Text

You can filter messages on the basis of their **subjects** or the text in the **message body.** To filter messages in these ways, enter a snippet of text in the Search For The Word(s) box. Then, using the In box, tell Outlook to search for the word(s) in the subject field only or in the subject field and message body.

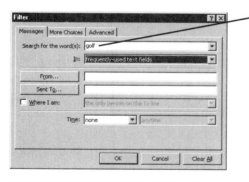

To see only messages that have something to do with golf, type the word *golf* in the Search For The Word(s) box.

Filtering Messages by Category

You can filter messages based on the **categories** you assigned them. Click the More Choices tab of the Filter dialog box. Click Categories, and then select the message categories you want in the Available Categories list. Click OK twice to filter the information viewer by category.

continues

Inbox Filters *(continued)*

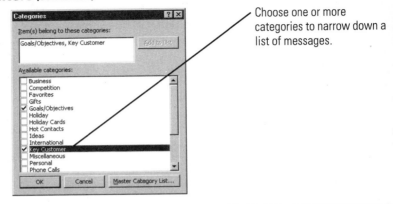

Choose one or more categories to narrow down a list of messages.

About the Clear All button and the Advanced tab

The Filter dialog box provides numerous other choices—let me quickly describe two of them before you're off to some other entry or you get back to doing real work. You can click Clear All to remove all of the filters in the Filter dialog box. And you can click the Advanced tab to display boxes and buttons for filtering messages even more precisely.

SEE ALSO   Filters; Task Filters; Views

Information Service

Outlook uses information services to send and receive **e-mail,** pass information between the **Outlook client** and an **Exchange server,** and get address information. If you want to send e-mail using an account with an **Internet service provider,** for example, you use an information service. If you want to connect to an Exchange server that's part of your local area network—perhaps so you can get a coworker's e-mail address from the **Global Address List** you use an information service.

Let me tell you three more quick things about information services. First, know that you don't install information services using Outlook or the Outlook setup program. You install an information service from a network server (like an Exchange server) or by using a separate disk that supplies an e-mail account setup program. Second, you can't use an information service until it's been added to your **profile.** Third, you look at, make minor changes to your computer's information services, and add services to your profile by using the Tools menu's Services command. (To do this, choose the Tools menu's Services command, click Add, and then when Outlook displays its list of installed services, double-click the name of the service you want to add.)

Information Store

The Information Store is where all of your **messages** and everyone else's messages get stored. Since we're on this topic, I should mention that in the special case when you're working on a network that includes an **Exchange server,** there are really two parts to the Information Store: the public Information Store and the private Information Store. The public Information Store holds messages stored in **Public Folders.** Anybody with permission can view a message in a Public Folder. The private Information Store holds messages stored in **Personal Folders.** The stuff stored in Personal Folders can be viewed only by the **sender** and the **recipient** of a message.

Information Viewer

The term *information viewer* refers to the right portion of the Outlook program window. The information viewer shows the **items** stored in the selected **folder.**

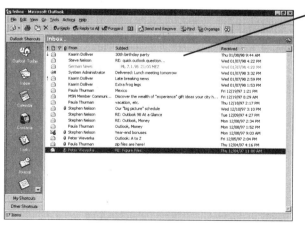

This is the information viewer.

SEE ALSO   Columns; Fields; Preview Pane

Internet

Once you understand that a **network** is just a bunch of computers that are connected so that information, including e-mail **messages,** can be shared, it's easy to understand what the Internet is: the Internet is a network of networks. The Internet may seem more appropriate as the topic of a U.S. Senate hearing or a story in a weekly news magazine, but it is important to Outlook users, too. Why? Because if you have an Internet connection (through an ISP, for example) or if your **organization's** network is connected to the Internet, you can easily send e-mail to anybody else connected to the Internet: the President of the United States, Bill Gates, or Mick Jagger. (You do need to know the recipient's **e-mail name,** however.)

SEE ALSO   Hyperlink; URL; World Wide Web

Internet Explorer SEE Microsoft Internet Explorer

Internet Service Provider

An Internet service provider, or ISP, is a company that lets you connect to its Internet host, usually for a fee. Once you're connected, your computer works either like a temporary Internet host or like a "dumb terminal" on which you can use the Internet by means of your connection to the provider's network. (When your computer works like a dumb terminal, you use your keyboard and your monitor, but it's really the other computer and its software that you're using.) People who talk about the Internet being an "information superhighway" like to say that Internet service providers are like on-ramps—they give you a way to get on the road.

One point that's a little bit confusing but important to understand is that you pay an Internet service provider merely to *access* the Internet. You're not paying anything to *use* the Internet. To go back to the on-ramps on the information superhighway analogy, Internet service providers set up tollbooths on the on-ramps that you must go through before you can get on the highway. But you actually use the highway for free.

Let me give you a few tips on picking an Internet service provider. First, check prices. You can pay anywhere from $10 to around $50 a month for an Internet service provider's service. (To keep your costs down, you'll probably want to choose a local provider to save on long-distance telephone charges.) Second, you should verify that you'll be able to connect when you want. (You can test this just by trying to connect a few times before you actually sign up.) Finally, you probably want to verify that your Internet service provider gives you access to the resources that interest you. (Some Internet service providers don't give you access to the more controversial and sensational newsgroups, for example.) So ask about access to whatever you're interested in.

SEE ALSO   Newsreader

Intranet

The **Internet,** it turns out, uses a bunch of special rules and conventions, called protocols, for sharing information and equipment. Because the Internet's protocols allow you to do some pretty neat things—including create Web pages—some **organizations** use these protocols on their own internal networks. Outsiders can't use these internal networks because these networks aren't part of the Internet. But because these internal networks work like the Internet, people call them intranets.

SEE ALSO   Hyperlink; URL; World Wide Web

Items

In Outlook, each **appointment, contact, Journal** entry, meeting, **message, Note,** or **task** is called an **item.** You can act upon items in a variety of ways: for example, you can **copy,** delete, **filter, forward, group,** move, print, send, and **sort** items.

Item-Specific Menu SEE Actions

Journal

The Journal is an **Outlook folder** that tracks your daily activities and displays them on a timeline. If the activity you want to track is an Outlook **item,** such as a phone call to a contact, you can tell the Journal to record it automatically. You can even have the Journal automatically record Microsoft Word documents, Microsoft Excel spreadsheets, and Microsoft Access databases that you create.

If you want to track an activity that has nothing whatever to do with Outlook, you can still use the Journal by adding entries to the Journal manually. So you could use the Journal to keep track of your off-track betting, for example. No, on second thought, forget that.

Journal entries appear as icons on the timeline. After you've recorded several activities, your Journal timeline appears something like the one shown below.

Using the Journal to Automatically Track Interactions with Contacts

Using the Journal, you can keep track of **e-mail** messages and faxes you send to and receive from selected **contacts.** You can also record meeting and task requests to and responses from your contacts.

To automatically record interactions with existing contacts, follow these steps:

1 Choose the Tools menu's Options command. Outlook displays the Options dialog box.

2 Click the Preferences tab, and then click Journal Options.

3 In the Automatically Record These Items box, check the items you want to automatically record in the Journal.

4 In the For These Contacts box, check the names of the contacts you want to record your interactions with.

5 Click OK. Outlook will make a Journal entry any time you interact in the indicated manner with any of the contacts you selected.

You can also elect to track contact activity when you add a contact. When you fill out the New Contact form, click the Journal tab.

Select this check box to automatically record Journal entries for interactions with the new contact.

Using the Journal to Record Documents You Create

To record any new files you create in other Microsoft Office programs, choose the Tools menu's Options command, click the Journal tab, and then check the names of the programs you want to track in the Also Record Files From box.

Using the Journal to Record Phone Calls to Contacts

Whenever you call a contact using Outlook's **AutoDial** feature, you can make a record of the phone call. This could come in handy for billing a customer for time spent on the phone, for instance, or simply to jog your memory later.

continues

Journal *(continued)*

To record a phone call to a contact, select the contact and choose the Actions menu's Call Contact command. Then choose the phone number you want to dial for the contact. Outlook displays the New Call dialog box.

Select this check box to record a Journal entry for a phone call.

Click Start Call, and Outlook displays the Call Status dialog box. Click Talk, pick up your phone, and Outlook displays the Phone Call form.

Click Start Timer to keep track of the length of the call. When the call is complete, click Pause Timer and click End Call. You can type notes about the call in the text area of the form either while the call is in progress or after you hang up. When you've finished writing notes, click the Save And Close toolbar button.

Manually Recording Outlook Items in the Journal

To manually record any Outlook item in the Journal, just drag the item to the Journal icon. Outlook displays the Journal Entry form for the item.

Fill in the text boxes to describe the meeting.

Manually Recording Miscellaneous Activities in the Journal

You can make a record of just about anything you want in the Journal. Display the Journal, and click the New Journal Entry toolbar button. Outlook displays the Untitled—Journal Entry form. Describe the entry type, and then fill out the rest of the boxes to describe the activity, event, or whatever. Then click the Save And Close toolbar button to record it in the Journal.

SEE ALSO   Contacts

Junk E-Mail

If you send mail over the **Internet,** sooner or later you're bound to get the electronic equivalent of junk mail. (You'll begin to get junk e-mail almost immediately, by the way, if you post messages to newsgroups.) To help you deal with junk e-mail, Outlook includes a special command, Add To Junk Senders List. This command tells Outlook to automatically delete any e-mail you get from a particular e-mail address or alias. To use this command, display the **Inbox,** right-click a junk e-mail message, and choose the Junk E-Mail command. Then choose the Junk E-Mail submenu's Add To Junk Senders List command. To add senders to your Adult Content Senders list, choose the Junk E-Mail submenu's Add To Adult Content Senders List command.

Outlook's Organize pane lets you create rules that tell Outlook what to do with the mail you receive from people on your Junk Senders and Adult Content Senders lists. You can tell Outlook to display junk e-mail messages in a different color or to automatically move these messages to another folder. To create such rules, display your Inbox and click the Organize toolbar button. Then click the Junk E-Mail tab.

continues

J

Junk E-Mail *(continued)*

Viewing Junk E-Mail Lists

To view your Junk Senders or Adult Content Senders lists, click the Junk E-Mail tab of the Organize pane. Then click the hyperlink to view more Junk E-Mail options. Click the Edit Junk Senders or Edit Adult Content Senders hyperlink to edit or remove senders on these lists.

Kilobit

A kilobit is 1,024 bits, which is relevant because modem speeds are usually measured in kilobits. Don't confuse the terms *kilobit* and *kilobyte*. It takes eight kilobits to make one kilobyte.

Kilobyte

I know you didn't buy this book to learn about the guts of your computer. But since I've used the term *kilobyte* in a couple of places, I thought I should at least define it. Okay? Good. A byte is an eight-digit string of 1s and 0s that your computer uses to represent a character. (These 1s and 0s are called bits.) This, for example, is a byte:

01010100

A kilobyte is roughly 1,000 of these bytes. (Or, to be excruciatingly precise, a kilobyte is exactly 1,024 of these bytes.)

Mailbox

If you're using Outlook as part of a network, a mailbox is the location on the server where your **messages** get delivered. Your network administrator sets up a mailbox for you and then you add the mailbox to your profile to view the messages in your mailbox.

Mail Folders

Mail folders include all the folders dealing with Outlook's **e-mail** functions—Inbox, Outbox, Sent Items, and Deleted Items. Messages you've received are stored in the **Inbox** folder. Messages you've sent are stored in the Sent Items folder. Messages you've sent that haven't yet been delivered to the **server** are stored in the Outbox folder. And, oh yes, there's another mail folder called

Deleted Items that stores messages you've deleted from the other
Mail folders. You may also have other Mail folders that you created
to store junk e-mail or a group of messages you want to set aside
and save in their own folder. You can open a Mail folder by
clicking its icon on the **Outlook Bar** or in the **Folder List.**

To see the
messages in a
folder, click its
icon.

Message

Messages are the communiqués you pass around with Outlook. The
joke you send to your boss. The birthday greeting to a friend who
works on the other side of the country. The electronic letter you
send to everyone in the sales department. What makes Outlook
special is that it artfully handles all of these items for you.

Writing a Message

To write a message, if you're already in the Inbox, click the New Mail Message
toolbar button. Otherwise, click the down-arrow next to the New Item toolbar
button (the button changes depending upon which Outlook folder you're in) to
display the New Item menu, and choose Mail Message. Outlook displays the
Message form. If you use the default Outlook e-mail text editor, your Message
form looks pretty much like the one shown in this figure.

continues

Message *(continued)*

1 Enter the **e-mail name** of the **recipient**.

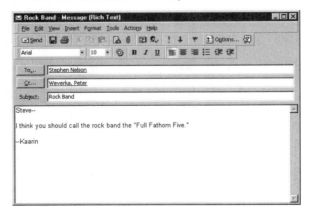

2 If you want someone else to get a **copy** of the message, enter his or her e-mail name.

3 Describe your message in a word or two. Or three.

4 Type your message text.

Click the Options tab to set general message options (such as **Importance**) and other delivery and tracking options.

Attaching a File to a Message

Many messages include only text typed in the Message form. But you can also **attach** a **file** to a message. In this way, you can include in your e-mail items such as word-processed documents, spreadsheets, and anything else you can store as a file on your hard disk. To attach a file, click the Insert File toolbar button. When Outlook displays the Insert File dialog box, name the file and identify its disk location.

Identify the file's disk location in the Look In box.

Enter the file's name in the File Name box.

Select an entry in the Files Of Type list box that specifies the types of files you want to see listed in the Insert File dialog box.

You have a choice

You get a choice as to the way Outlook attaches a file to your message. If your file contains only unformatted text and you just want to plunk the text in your message, click the Text Only option button. (It tells Outlook to insert the file as a text file in your message—something you would do only with text files.) If your file contains more than unformatted text, click either the Attachment or the Shortcut option button. Clicking Attachment tells Outlook to insert an actual copy of the file in the message. The Shortcut option is available only for messages created using Microsoft Outlook Rich Text mail format. The Shortcut option inserts a shortcut icon in your message that points to a file on a computer. When Outlook later sends the message, it uses this shortcut to find the file with the actual message. (The recipient must have access to the location where the file is stored.)

Attaching Other Items to a Message

You can attach any existing Outlook item to a message. In other words, you can insert other messages, **Calendar** files, **Contacts** list items, **Notes,** and so forth. To do this, choose the Insert menu's Item command. When Outlook displays the Insert Item dialog box, identify the item you want to send and tell Outlook how you want it inserted.

Identify the item's folder in the Look In box.

Click OK to insert the item.

Select the item in the Items box.

Sending a Message Over a Local Area Network

After you write a message, send it by clicking the Send toolbar button. If your computer connects to a network that includes an **Exchange server,** Outlook sends your message to the recipient you named. In a few minutes—maybe sooner—he or she receives the message. (Although how long it will take the recipient to read it is anybody's guess.)

continues

Message *(continued)*

Sending a Message Over the Internet

If your computer connects to the **Internet** and that's how you send and receive messages, clicking the Send toolbar button tells Outlook to place the message in your Outbox folder. To move the message out of your Outbox and to the mail server you use to send and receive e-mail, click the Send And Receive toolbar button. Or, alternatively, if you have more than one **Internet service provider** and you want to select one for sending the message, choose the Tools menu's Send And Receive command. When Outlook displays the Send And Receive submenu, choose the Internet service provider you want to use from the submenu. Outlook makes the connection to the Internet service provider and then sends and receives any Internet e-mail messages.

Reading Your Messages

To read the messages that other people have sent you, display the **Inbox** folder by clicking its icon on the **Outlook Bar.** Outlook lists any messages you've received. Unread messages are displayed in boldface. To view a message, double-click it. When you do this, Outlook displays the message in its own window.

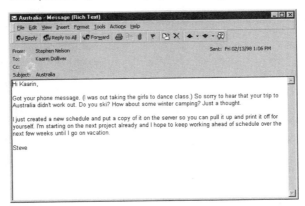

When you finish reading a message, just close the window. This tells Outlook to save the message in your Inbox folder and not do anything else with it. Alternatively, you can click the Delete toolbar button. This tells Outlook to move the message to the Deleted Items folder. (Presumably, you move messages to the Deleted Items folder as a last stop before you zap them forever by choosing the Tools menu's Empty "Deleted Items" Folder command.)

Replying to a Message

It's easy to reply to messages that others have sent you. To do this, click either the Reply or the Reply To All toolbar buttons. The Reply toolbar button tells Outlook you want to send a message only to the person who originally sent the message to you. The Reply To All toolbar button tells Outlook you want to send a message to the original sender and to everyone else who received a copy of the message. After you click either the Reply or Reply To All toolbar buttons, Outlook opens a new Message form that holds a copy of the original message and names the recipients to whom you want to send the message. Type your reply, and click the Send toolbar button.

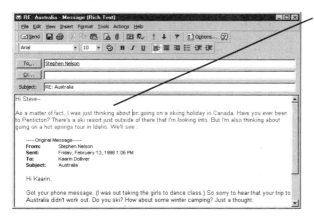

Whatever you type in your reply message gets inserted here.

Forwarding a Message

It's easy to forward a message you received from someone else. First either select the message in the Outlook window by clicking it or display the message in a separate window. Next click the Forward toolbar button. Outlook opens a Message form that holds a copy of the original message.

Specify to whom you want to forward the message by entering the e-mail name. (Click To to open your **Address Book.**)

continues

Message *(continued)*

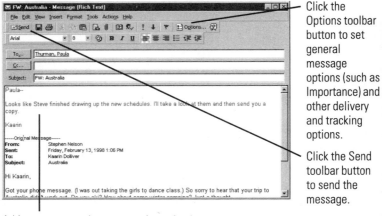

Click the Options toolbar button to set general message options (such as Importance) and other delivery and tracking options.

Click the Send toolbar button to send the message.

Add comments to the message by typing here.

Printing a Message

You can print the messages you write and receive. To do this, just select the message and click the Print toolbar button.

If you want more control over how your message is printed, choose the File menu's Print command. When Outlook displays the Print dialog box, choose a printer, tell Outlook how many copies to print, describe what Outlook should do about any attachments, and so forth.

Message Body

The message body is the actual message. In other words, it's the text element of the message, not the **e-mail name** of the **sender** or the **recipient** or the message **subject**.

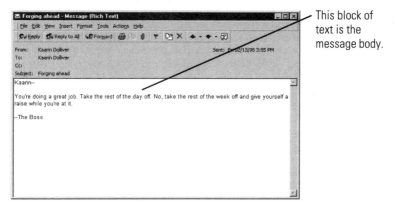

This block of text is the message body.

Message Expiration

You can tell Outlook that a message should expire if a recipient hasn't read it by a certain date or time. In other words, you can say, "Okay, deliver this message—but if the recipient doesn't read it by some point in the future, just make the message unavailable for reading." To set an expiration date for a message, display the message in a Message form and click the Options toolbar button. When Outlook displays the Message Options dialog box, select the Expires After check box and specify the expiration date.

Enter the expiration date here.

Message Flag

When you flag a message, you mark it with a flag icon, either to remind yourself to take further action or to ask someone else to act. Message flags appear in two places: as a message bar added to the **Message form** itself and in the Flag Status **column** of the Message view of the Inbox **information viewer.**

The message flag appears here.

Outlook has several predefined message flags: Call, Follow Up, Forward, Read, Reply, Reply To All, or Review. Or you can invent a message flag of your own. You can also set a due date by which you want the suggested action taken.

Flagging a Message

To flag a message, open an existing message or click the New Mail Message toolbar button. Then click the Flag For Follow Up toolbar button. Outlook displays the Flag For Follow Up dialog box.

Select a flag from this box.

Click Clear Flag to remove a flag previously set.

To set a reminder date, enter it here.

Message Form

The Message form is the window Outlook displays that you can
use to write **e-mail messages.** Why it's called a **form** instead of a
window is sometimes confusing. But all you need to understand is
that Outlook calls the windows you use to enter information—such
as an e-mail message—forms. In the case of an e-mail message,
"form" doesn't fit the bill very well. For the **custom forms** that
Outlook lets you create, however, "form" works quite nicely. You
can create forms, for example, for reporting employee business
expenses. (In this case, employees would fill out business expense
forms and e-mail them to Mildred in accounts payable.)

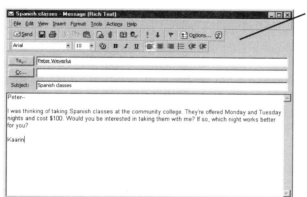

This is the
Message form.
You can also
call it the
Message Form
window.

Message Format

Outlook gives you four different choices for the editor you use to
create new e-mail messages: HTML, Microsoft Outlook Rich Text,
Plain Text, and Microsoft Word. The editor you choose determines
the message formatting options you have available. To select a message editor, choose the Tools menu's Options command and click
the Mail Format tab. Then select an editor in the Message Format
drop-down list box.

But which editor should you choose? Well, it depends on the e-mail
setups of the people with whom you most regularly communicate.
For example, if you know that most of your message recipients have
newer e-mail programs that can read HTML-formatted mail, you
might want to choose HTML so that you can make use of Outlook's
stationery. HTML format has one major drawback, however. If a

continues

93

Message Format *(continued)*

recipient's e-mail software can't read HTML-formatted mail, when the recipient displays the message, it is littered with HTML code, which can sometimes be annoying.

Microsoft Outlook Rich Text is a good option for many people because it allows you to add some simple formatting, and unlike HTML, Microsoft Outlook Rich Text–formatted messages can be read by older e-mail programs. Plain Text, as its name conveys, is as simple as it gets. When you write messages in Plain Text format, none of the options on the Formatting toolbar is available. While this is a disadvantage, there is one big advantage to Plain Text–formatted messages—they translate well regardless of the recipient's Internet connection, e-mail software, or operating system. If you use Microsoft Word as your e-mail editor, you can use features from Word, such as tables and highlighting in your messages. You also have more options for formatting messages you receive. But using Word as your e-mail editor means that Outlook opens a copy of Word every time you write a message. And this uses memory and could slow you down.

Message Header

The message header lists the **sender, recipient,** message **subject,** and a bunch of other information. All you really need to know about the message header is this: if you right-click different parts of the message header, such as the sender name, you access a shortcut menu of commands that you can use to do neat things.

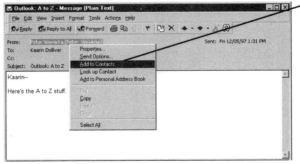

When you right-click one of the recipient names in the message header, Outlook displays a shortcut menu with a command for adding the person to your **Contacts** folder.

Message Options

You can provide general instructions to Outlook concerning how to save, send, receive, and track messages. To specify these instructions in one fell swoop, choose the Tools menu's Options command, click the Preferences tab, and then click E-Mail Options. When Outlook displays the E-Mail Options dialog box, use the boxes and buttons to change the way e-mail messages are handled.

Click Advanced E-Mail Options to display a dialog box that lets you describe how Outlook saves, sends, and receives messages.

Click Tracking Options to display a dialog box that lets you specify how Outlook tracks messages sent over a local area network using an **Exchange server**.

You can also set options individually for each message as you write it. To do this, click the Options toolbar button in the Message form as you compose a message. Incidentally, if you've set mail options in the E-Mail Options dialog box, the settings you make for individual messages override the general ones.

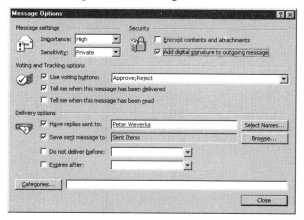

SEE ALSO Delivery Receipt; Importance; Read Receipt; Sensitivity

Message Subject SEE Subject

Microsoft Internet Explorer

Outlook comes with a copy of Microsoft's Web browser, Internet Explorer. Using Internet Explorer, you can view Web pages and even access other Internet resources.

SEE ALSO   Outlook Express

Microsoft Schedule+

Microsoft Schedule+ is another time-management components of the Exchange family of products. Using Schedule+, you can schedule appointments and meetings, keep a to-do list, and organize projects. Because you can do all of these things in Outlook as well, you don't need Schedule+. But you should know that if you used Schedule+ with Exchange and you're hooked on it, you can still use it as your main scheduling program. To do this, choose the Tools menu's Options command, click the Preferences tab, click Calendar Options, and then select the Use Microsoft Schedule+ As My Primary Calendar check box.

Microsoft Word

If you have Microsoft Word 97, you can use Word as your e-mail editor and call on the power of Word to help you write your messages. To tell Outlook you want to use Word as your e-mail editor, choose the Tools menu's Options command. On the Mail Format tab, select Microsoft Word from the Send In This Message Format drop-down list box. The next time you open a New Message window, Outlook displays a little message box to alert you that it is opening Word as your e-mail editor. If you look carefully, you can see that the Message form now includes extra buttons on the toolbars. (You might recognize these buttons from Word.) You can use these buttons to edit and format your e-mail messages.

MIME

MIME stands for "multipurpose **Internet** mail extensions." MIME is a protocol that lets you attach binary **files** to **e-mail** messages and send these over the Internet. As long as the people to whom you send messages also have e-mail readers that support the MIME protocol and the mail servers you and your recipients use support the MIME protocol, others can extract and use the files you send them. For example, using MIME, someone can attach a Microsoft Word document to an e-mail message. If the recipient's e-mail reader supports MIME, the recipient can save the Word document in the e-mail message. If the recipient has a copy of Word for Windows, he or she can open and work with the document in Word.

While Outlook understands and supports the MIME protocol, not all e-mail clients and servers do. For this reason, sometimes you can't use MIME. Sometimes you need to use **Uuencode.**

NetMeeting

Microsoft Internet Explorer and the full installation of Outlook come with a conferencing program called NetMeeting. NetMeeting lets you audio-conference or video-conference with another person over the Internet. To make full use of NetMeeting, you need speakers, a microphone, and optionally, a video camera.

Using Outlook to Store NetMeeting Information

When you create contact items, you can enter NetMeeting information for the contact by clicking the Details tab of the Contact form. Enter the name of the directory server over which the Internet calls with the contact take place in the Directory Server text box. Enter the contact's e-mail alias in the E-Mail Alias text box.

To create a NetMeeting appointment in the Calendar, create an appointment item in the usual way and then select the This Is An Online Meeting check box. Click the Online tab to enter a server for the meeting location and the e-mail address of the meeting organizer.

To organize an online meeting yourself and send meeting requests to other attendees, choose the Actions menu's New Online Meeting Request command.

continues

NetMeeting *(continued)*

Starting NetMeeting

You can place a NetMeeting call to a contact by selecting the contact in your Contacts folder and choosing the Actions menu's Call Using NetMeeting command. You can place a NetMeeting call to someone on one of your other Address Book lists by choosing the Go menu's Internet Call command and the Internet Call submenu's From Address Book command. You can also open NetMeeting by choosing the Go menu's Internet Call command and the Internet Call submenu's Internet Call command.

SEE ALSO   Plan A Meeting Wizard

Network

A network is just a bunch of computers that are hooked together so that the people who use the computers can share information. If you're using Outlook to send e-mail to coworkers, by the way, your computer is connected to a network.

SEE ALSO   Internet; Intranet

Newsgroup SEE Newsreader

Newsreader

Outlook 98 comes with a program called Outlook Express News, which is an Internet newsreader. Newsreaders let you read e-mail messages that people have posted to newsgroups. (A newsgroup works like an electronic bulletin board.) Using Outlook Express News, you can also post your own messages to newsgroups.

Installing Outlook Express News

You install Outlook Express News at the same time that you install Outlook. To configure Outlook Express News so that it works with your **Internet service provider's** newsgroup server, you may need to run the Connection Wizard. Or, alternatively, you may need to get and then follow whatever configuration instructions your Internet service provider supplies.

Starting Outlook Express News

You can start Outlook Express News by choosing Microsoft Outlook Newsreader from your Programs menu. You can also start Outlook Express News from within Outlook by choosing the Go menu's News command.

Previewing a Newsgroup

To check out the messages posted to a newsgroup, follow these steps:

1 Select the server that stores the newsgroup from the list on the left.

2 Click the Newsgroups toolbar button. Outlook Express News displays the Newsgroups dialog box.

3 Scroll through the list of newsgroups on the server until you see one that interests you. Or type a keyword in the text box to shorten the list of available newsgroups to ones that include the keyword in their name.

4 Click Go To.

Subscribing to a Newsgroup

To add a newsgroup to your newsgroup list so that you can easily visit the newsgroup on future occasions, you need to subscribe to the newsgroup. Subscribing doesn't cost you anything; it just allows you to access the newsgroup more quickly. To subscribe to a newsgroup you are previewing, right-click its name and choose the shortcut menu's Subscribe To This Newsgroup command. To subscribe to a newsgroup that isn't displayed in your newsgroup list, follow these steps:

1 Select the server that stores the newsgroup from the list on the left.

2 Click the Newsgroups toolbar button to display the Newsgroups dialog box.

3 Double-click the newsgroup to which you want to subscribe. (You can subscribe to multiple newsgroups by repeating this step.)

continues

Newsreader *(continued)*

Unsubscribing from a Newsgroup

To unsubscribe from a newsgroup, start Outlook Express News. If necessary, expand the Folder List to show all the newsgroups to which you subscribe. Then right-click the newsgroup, and choose the shortcut menu's Unsubscribe From This Newsgroup command.

Reading Messages

To read a message in a newsgroup, select the newsgroup in the Folder List pane. Outlook Express News displays the message headers for the newsgroup's messages in the Message List pane. Click a message to display it in the Preview pane. If you double-click a message, Outlook Express News displays the message in its own window.

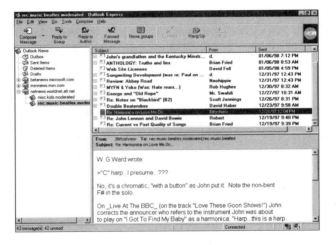

Reading messages offline

The above procedure for reading messages works only if you are currently working online. For most people, staying online while working in Outlook Express News is usually the easiest way to read newsgroup messages. However, I should tell you that with Outlook Express News, you can also select the messages and headers you want to read, download them to your computer, and then read them offline.

Reading an Attachment

Some messages include encoded attachments. Typically, you don't have to do anything special to read or save an attachment. If you open a message that includes a graphics image, for example, Outlook Express News decodes the attachment and then displays the image in the Preview pane. If you open a message that includes another type of attachment—perhaps a program file, for example—Outlook Express News decodes the attachment and then displays a shortcut icon for the file in the Preview pane. To save an attachment to your hard disk, right-click the image or its icon. Then choose the shortcut menu's Save As command.

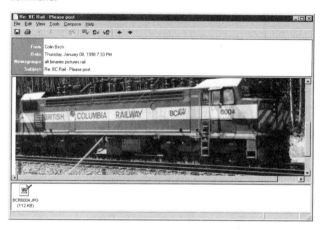

Stopping downloads of large messages

Large messages, such as those that include attachments, can take time to download. If you want to tell Outlook Express News to stop downloading a message, click the Stop toolbar button.

Working with Multipart Messages

Sometimes an attachment is too large to fit within a single message. When this is the case, the person posting the file splits the attachment across several messages, usually labeled something like 1 of 3, 2 of 3, and 3 of 3. To decode and then save an attachment that has been split across multiple messages, select the messages that hold the attachment. Then right-click the selection, and choose the shortcut menu's Combine And Decode command. When Outlook Express News displays the Combine And Decode dialog box, click Move Up or Move Down to arrange the messages in the correct order. Then click OK.

continues

Newsreader *(continued)*

Posting Messages

To post a message in a newsgroup, click the newsgroup item in the Folder List pane. Then click the Compose Message toolbar button. When Outlook Express News displays a Message form, type your message and click Post.

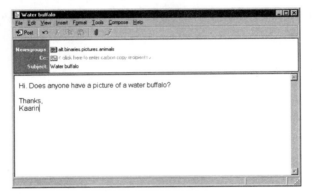

Posting Messages with Attachments

If you want to include an attachment with your message, click the Insert File toolbar button. (This button appears on the Message form's toolbar.) When Outlook Express News displays the Insert Attachment dialog box, identify the folder that holds the file in the Look In drop-down list box. Double-click the file in the list box to attach it to the message.

Notes

Notes is one of the **Outlook folders,** and Notes themselves are just like, well, electronic sticky notes. You can use an Outlook Note to write down a phone number, an address, a quick to-do list—all the things you put on paper notes. As you can with the paper kind, you can stick one of these Notes on your desktop where it will serve as a reminder to you—until you get around to filing it more permanently or tossing it in the trash.

Creating a Note

Creating a Note is simple. Just display the Notes folder, and click the New Note toolbar button. A blank Note pops up on your screen. Type the text you want to remember, and click the Note's Close button, and you've created a Note.

Click the X to close a Note and add it to the Notes list.

Customizing a Note

Click the icon in the Note's upper left corner to display the Note's Control menu. Choose the Control menu's Color command to change the Note's color. Choose **Categories** to assign the Note to a category.

continues

N

Notes *(continued)*

Working with Notes

Whenever you use the Taskbar to switch to another application, you always minimize any visible Notes. If you close or minimize all other applications, you can leave a Note on your desktop so you'll see it the next time you glance at your screen.

Once you type something on a Note, you enable the Cut and Copy commands on the Control menu. Then you can paste part or all of the Note into a message or wherever else you want. You can paste the Clipboard's contents into a Note by choosing the Paste command from the Control menu.

Moving and Resizing a Note

To resize a Note, click and drag its edges as you would any other object. Or right-click the bar at the top of the Note, and choose the shortcut menu's Minimize or Maximize commands. Click and drag the Note's top bar to move the Note anywhere on the screen.

Keeping Track of Notes

To print a Note, choose the Control menu's Print command. Choose the Control menu's Save As command to save a Note to a folder anywhere on your hard disk. To forward a Note, choose the Control menu's **Forward** command. Outlook opens a Forward **Message form** so that you can send the Note anywhere you can send **e-mail.**

When you close a Note, it is automatically posted to the Notes folder. To view the Notes folder, click the Notes icon on the **Outlook Bar** or in the **Folder List.** You can **group** Notes as you would any other Outlook items. You can define **views** for the Notes list and use all the other **information viewer** features such as **sorting** and **filtering.**

Deleting a Note

To delete a Note, select it in the Notes list and click the Delete toolbar button.

Color-coding your Notes

By changing the color of Notes, you can code them. For example, make all of your phone number Notes yellow and all your reminders blue. Or use whatever combination you like. To change the color of a Note, right-click it in the Notes window, choose the shortcut menu's Color command, and then choose a color from the submenu.

Office Assistant

If you installed the full version of Outlook, whenever you click the Office Assistant toolbar button or choose the Help menu's Microsoft Outlook Help command, an animated help guru called the Office Assistant pops up. To use the Office Assistant, type your question in the box provided. Then click Search, and the Assistant displays a list of Help topics that most closely relate to your question. To read a topic, click its button.

When the Office Assistant has a tip for you, it displays a lightbulb icon. Click the lightbulb to read the tip.

Type your question here.

Offline Folders

An offline folder is a copy of the server folder that Outlook uses to actually deliver and store **messages.** If you use an offline folder—say you're not currently connected to the **network**—you periodically need to get it updated by **synchronizing** your files. First, however, you'll need to reconnect to the network.

SEE ALSO   Remote Mail

Online Service SEE Internet Service Provider

Organization

According to Outlook, an organization is a bunch of **Exchange servers** and Outlook **clients** that work happily together. In a little company, the organization might consist of a single server and half a dozen clients. In a big company, the organization might consist of dozens of servers and hundreds of clients scattered across multiple sites.

Organize Pane

When you click the Organize toolbar button, Outlook opens the
Organize pane. You can use the Organize pane to accomplish several tasks. You can use it to move items from one folder to another,
to change the view of a folder, or to categorize items, for example. If
you're looking at your Inbox folder and you click the Organize
toolbar button, Outlook displays boxes and buttons that let you
move messages to another message folder, use different colors for
messages from different people, change your **view** of your Inbox,
and create rules for handling junk e-mail. Other folders provide
similar boxes and buttons for moving and rearranging their items.

Click a hyperlink
that describes
how you want
to organize the
folder's items.

Describe how
you want to
organize the
folder's items in
these boxes.

Using the Organize Pane to Move Items to Other Folders

You can use the Organize pane to move an item you specify to a folder you specify.
If you choose to move the item to a different type of folder, Outlook automatically
creates a new type of item for you. For example, if you choose to move a task from
your Tasks list to your Calendar, Outlook creates a new appointment from the task.
To use the Organize pane to move items, follow these steps:

1 Select the item you want to move to a different folder.

2 Click the Using Folders hyperlink.

3 Identify the folder you want to receive the new items by using the first drop-down list box. (The name of this list box differs depending on the folder you're in.)

4 Click Move.

5 In your Mail and Deleted Items folders, you have the option of creating a rule that moves all messages to or from the contact you specify to another folder.

Using the Organize Pane to Create New Categories

You can also use the Organize pane to create new categories for items in your Calendar, Tasks, or Journal folders. To do this, select the item or items you want to categorize and then click the Organize toolbar button.

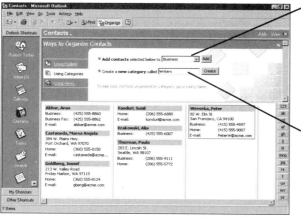

To add the selected item to an existing category, specify the category here and then click Add.

To create a new category for selected item, enter it here and then click Create.

SEE ALSO   AutoCreate

Outlook Bar

The Outlook Bar lets you move around not only among the various **Outlook folders** but around your entire computer and even your local network. You can use the Outlook Bar and its **shortcut icons** in place of the Outlook **Folder List** to navigate within Outlook; furthermore, you can use it like Windows Explorer or My Computer to access any folder on your hard drive, other network drives, or on the Internet. And if there's a folder or **Web page** you find yourself accessing frequently, you can place a shortcut to it on the Outlook Bar.

Using the Outlook Bar to Navigate with Outlook

To move to an Outlook folder, click its icon on the Outlook Bar.

Click the **Calendar** icon to display the Calendar.

Click My Shortcuts to display a group of folders related to **e-mail.**

If you click My Shortcuts, Outlook displays this set of shortcut icons.

Click The Sent Items icon to display all the e-mail items you've sent recently.

The Outlook Bar's Group buttons

If you used Outlook 97, you may have noticed that you don't have the Outlook Shortcuts, My Shortcuts, and Other Shortcuts buttons on your Outlook Bar as described in this book. Your buttons retained their names from the previous version of Outlook and are called Outlook, Mail, and Other. While the names are a little different, the group of icons available when you click one of these buttons is pretty much the same. That much said, if you get confused by the explanations in this book and want to rename your Group buttons, just right-click a button and choose the shortcut menu's Rename Group command. You can also create your own new group by right-clicking the Outlook Bar and choosing the shortcut menu's Add New Group command. Then add folder icons to the group by dragging them from the Folder List to the Outlook Bar.

Accessing My Computer, Other Folders, and the Internet Using the Outlook Bar

Click Other Shortcuts to display the My Computer, My Documents, and **Favorites** shortcut icons. The Favorites folder contains the Internet addresses you've selected as your favorites while browsing the **World Wide Web.** Just click an icon to launch your **Web browser** and the Web page you selected.

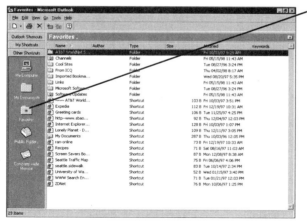

Click the Favorites icon to display the contents of the Favorites folder.

continues

O

Outlook Bar *(continued)*

Customizing the Outlook Bar

To add an Outlook Bar shortcut icon that points to your favorite folder, follow these steps:

1 Click Other Shortcuts on the Outlook Bar.

2 Click the My Computer icon to display the folder hierarchy.

3 Find the folder to which you want to create a shortcut, and right-click it.

4 Choose the shortcut menu's Add To Outlook Bar command.

What's the big deal?

Why the fuss over the Outlook Bar when you can just use Windows Explorer to navigate the folder hierarchy? Good question. You might not want to use the Outlook Bar in this manner. However, if you're using Outlook to send and receive e-mail, check your schedule, and keep track of your contacts, you'll probably be spending a lot of time there. And this means you may find Outlook and its Outlook Bar much faster and more convenient than Windows Explorer or the Start menu.

Outlook Client

On a network, the messaging system really consists of two components: the Outlook client and the **Exchange server.** The Outlook client is a program that runs on your computer; the Exchange Server program runs on another computer. This Field Guide doesn't examine the server component of the messaging system except in passing. The server component of Outlook is the concern of the network **administrator.**

Outlook Express

Microsoft Internet Explorer 4 comes with a "lite" version of Outlook called Outlook Express. So that's what Outlook Express is—basically just a scaled-down version of Outlook. Unfortunately, there is a somewhat confusing twist to the relationship between Outlook and Outlook Express, which I'll mention because we're already on the subject. It turns out that Outlook Express comes with a **newsreader.** And Outlook shares this newsreader, called Outlook Express News.

Outlook Folders

This group of **folders** includes the Outlook Item folders: **Calendar, Contacts, Inbox, Journal, Notes,** and **Tasks.** You can open an Outlook folder by clicking its icon on the **Outlook Bar** or in the **Folder List.**

SEE ALSO   Mail Folders

Outlook Item SEE Item

Outlook Today

If you click the Outlook Today shortcut icon, Outlook displays a special, summary view of the items stored in your folders. This summary view lists new e-mail messages you've received, Calendar appointments or events you've scheduled for the current week, and tasks you've indicated you want to finish for the current week.

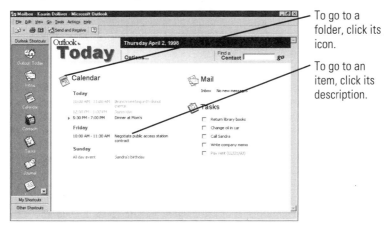

To go to a folder, click its icon.

To go to an item, click its description.

Out Of Office Assistant

If you use Outlook as a client for an **Exchange server,** you can use Outlook's Out Of Office Assistant to automatically reply to **messages** that people send. In this way, you can let people know, for example, that you're on vacation for two weeks. Or you can let people know that you are in meetings all day and cannot respond to messages in a timely manner.

Creating a Standard Response

To create a standard response that the Out Of Office Assistant can use to reply to every message you receive, choose the Tools menu's Out Of Office Assistant command. Outlook displays the Out Of Office Assistant dialog box.

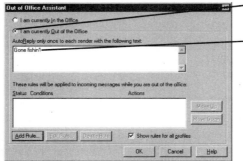

Click here to indicate that you're out of your office.

Type a standard reply to all messages that arrive while you're away.

Using Rules and Actions

You may not want to handle all the incoming messages you receive when out of the office in the same way. If you want to be more specific, you can define rules that tell the Out Of Office Assistant how to monitor incoming messages and what to do when it sees a message you want processed in a certain way. To define rules such as these, follow these steps:

1 Choose the Tools menu's Out Of Office Assistant command.

2 Click Add Rule. Outlook displays the Edit Rule dialog box.

3 Enter the sender name or recipient name whose messages you want the Out Of Office Assistant to look for, using semicolons to separate multiple names. (Click Check Names to verify the spelling of names.)

4 Select the Sent Directly To Me or Copied (Cc) To Me check boxes to tell the Out Of Office Assistant to look for messages sent directly to you or only copied to you.

5 Enter text in the Subject and Message Body boxes to tell the Out Of Office Assistant to look for messages that include specific words or phrases, using semicolons to separate words or phrases. Here, for example, I'm looking for messages relating to the upcoming company picnic. (I'll tell Outlook to forward those messages to Steve.)

6 After defining the rules for monitoring your incoming messages, tell the Out Of Office Assistant what actions to take when it finds a message that meets the conditions described by your rules. To describe these rules, select the Edit Rule dialog box's Perform These Actions options, which are described in the table that follows on the next page:

continues

O

Office Assistant *(continued)*

Action	Description
Alert With	Out Of Office Assistant displays a pop-up message (with text you supply) or makes a sound. (Specify whether you want the pop-up message or the sound by clicking Action.)
Delete	Moves the message to your Deleted Items folder.
Move To	Moves the message to another **folder**. (Specify the folder by clicking Folder.)
Copy To	Makes a copy of the message, and places it in another folder. (Specify this other folder by clicking Folder.)
Forward	Forwards the message to another user. (Specify the user by entering a name in the text box.)
Reply With	Replies to the message with a standard response. (Specify the standard response by clicking Template to open a New Message form, and then type your response.)
Custom	Responds to the message with a customized response. (Ask the **administrator** about these.)

After you define the rules and describe the actions that the Out Of Office Assistant should take when it sees a message that, according to your rules, is one you're interested in, click OK and the Out Of Office Assistant begins its work. Whenever you activate the Out Of Office Assistant and it then sees an interesting message, it performs whatever action you specified. Click Move Up or Move Down in the Out Of Office Assistant dialog box to prioritize the rules and actions you specify.

About the Advanced options

You can establish additional rules by clicking Advanced and using the Advanced dialog box's options. Its options let you tell the Out Of Office Assistant to look for messages with **attachments,** messages of a certain size, and messages that *don't* meet the conditions you specify. (Usually the Out Of Office Assistant looks for messages that do meet the conditions you specify.)

SEE ALSO   **Rules Wizard**

PAB SEE Personal Address Book

Paragraph Alignment SEE Alignment

Permission

Within an Exchange **organization,** the term *permission* refers to the ability to access items in a **Public Folder.** To read or place a **post** in a Public Folder, you must have permission. (The **administrator** gives permission.)

SEE ALSO   Delegate Access

Personal Address Book

In Microsoft Exchange, you used a Personal Address Book to create a personal list of people's **e-mail names** (and a whole bunch of other information as well). Because you may have used a previous Microsoft e-mail client, therefore, Outlook happily lets you work with Personal Address Books. In fact, in most cases when you add someone's name and e-mail address to the **Address Book,** for example, you actually get to choose whether that information goes into a Personal Address Book or the **Contacts** folder.

Don't confuse the Personal Address Book with the Address Book tool, by the way. The Address Book is a tool you use to view the contents of all the different places you store name and address information: a Personal Address Book, the Contacts folder, and if you're working on a network that includes an **Exchange server,** a Global Address List.

To view the contents of your Personal Address Book, click the Address Book toolbar button. When Outlook displays the Address Book window, select Personal Address Book in the Show Names From The list.

Personal Folder

A Personal Folder is just a folder you use to store the items you create in Outlook and the messages you receive. Other users on your **network** can't read the messages in your Personal Folders unless you give them **delegate access** permission to do so.

SEE ALSO   Public Folder

Plan A Meeting Wizard

Outlook's Plan A Meeting Wizard helps you schedule meetings.
When you open your **Calendar** and choose the **Actions** menu's
Plan A Meeting command, Outlook displays the Plan A Meeting
dialog box. Outlook checks your schedule and the schedules of the
prospective attendees and finds a time slot that appears as free time
on everyone's schedule.

Planning a Meeting

To schedule a meeting from the Calendar folder, choose the Options menu's Plan A
Meeting command. Outlook displays the Plan A Meeting dialog box. Your name
appears on the first line of the All Attendees list. Choose the day of the meeting by
clicking a date in the Meeting Start Time drop-down calendar. Pick a tentative
meeting time and duration by dragging the green and red selection bars.

To add an attendee, click
Invite Others and select
people from your **Address
Book**.

Busy times show up in blue
on this schedule.

Click AutoPick to find the
next available time slot that's
free for all attendees.

Click Make Meeting to add
the meeting to your Calendar
and to send invitations (in the
form of **e-mail messages**) to
the prospective attendees.

SEE ALSO   NetMeeting

Pocket Outlook

Microsoft sells a special version of Outlook called Pocket Outlook
for palmtop computers that use Windows CE. If you use Pocket
Outlook, you can synchronize and share Pocket Outlook's information with Outlook's information. (This means, for example, that
you can use Pocket Outlook when you travel and use Outlook in
your office.)

Post

A post is a special type of **message** that doesn't get delivered to a **recipient,** but gets delivered to a **Public Folder.** In effect, posts are very much like the announcements tacked on the bulletin board at the local grocery store. You know the type I mean: the ones that advertise 13-year-old baby-sitters, '69 Camaros, and rewards for lost Labradors.

Posts are a slick way to share information with other Outlook **users** without having to send everybody an individual message. By having a Public Folder that stores, for example, one copy of a company's holiday schedule, holiday information is always available to everybody and is easy to get.

Creating a Public Folder for Posting Information

To create a Public Folder for posts, select the Public Folders folder, choose the File menu's New command, and then choose the New submenu's Folder command. When Outlook displays the Create New Folder dialog box, name the new folder, identify its contents, specify its location in the folder hierarchy, describe it briefly, and click OK. (You must have **permission** to do this.)

Writing a Post

To write a post, select the Public Folder to which you want to post the information. Then click the New Post In This Folder toolbar button. When you click this button, Outlook probably displays an Untitled Discussion form that resembles the Message form. But if the person who created the Public Folder intends for you to use a different form for posts in the folder, the form you see may look a little different. For example, the folder creator might have designed a custom form for posts in that folder or might have told Outlook to use a different Outlook form, such as the Contact form, for posts in the folder. To select a different form for your post, choose the Tools menu's Forms command and the Forms submenu's Choose Form command. To post a message using the Discussion form, follow the steps on the next page:

continues

Post *(continued)*

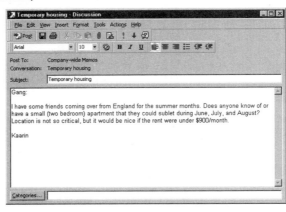

1 Describe your message in a word or two.

2 Type your message text here.

3 Assign your message to a category.

Attaching Outlook Items to a Post

You can attach any Outlook **item** to a post. To do this, choose the Insert menu's Item command. When Outlook displays the Insert Item dialog box, identify the item you want to send.

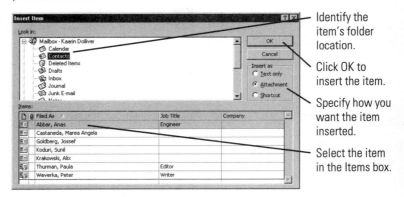

Identify the item's folder location.

Click OK to insert the item.

Specify how you want the item inserted.

Select the item in the Items box.

Sending a Post

After you write a post, send it by clicking the Post toolbar button. Outlook places your post in the folder you selected.

Posting a File

You can attach a file to a post in the same way you attach a file to any other Outlook item. You do this by clicking the Insert File toolbar button or by choosing the Insert menu's File command. But an easier way of sharing files in Public Folders is by posting the files on their own. This way they don't get lost or overlooked in messages. To post a file to a Public Folder, just click Other Shortcuts on the Outlook Bar and then click My Computer to locate the file you want to post. When you find the file, drag it to the Public Folder icon on the Outlook Bar or in your **Folder List.**

Reading a Post

To read a post in a Public Folder, display the folder's contents list by clicking the folder's icon in the Folder List. Outlook lists any posts in the folder. To view a post, double-click it. When you do this, Outlook displays the post.

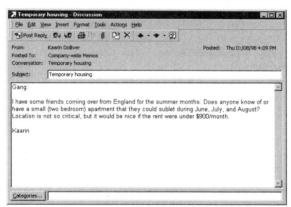

Group post messages by conversation topic

The easiest way to review posts that were created in response to an original post is to group them by **conversation thread.** To do this, display the folder with the posts you want to view, choose the View menu's Current View command, and then choose the Current View submenu's By Conversation Topic command.

Replying to a Post

You can reply to a post in either of two ways: by replying directly to the post sender or by sending another post.

continues

Post *(continued)*

To reply directly to the sender, click the Post Reply toolbar button. Outlook opens a New Message form that contains a copy of the original post. Type your reply, and click the Send toolbar button.

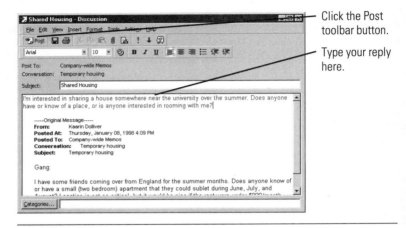

Click the Post toolbar button.

Type your reply here.

Forwarding a Post

If you read a post that you want to forward to someone else, you can easily do so. First either select the post in the **information viewer** or display the post in its own window. Next click the Forward toolbar button. Outlook opens a New Message form that contains a copy of the original post.

Specify to whom you want to forward the post by entering an **e-mail name.**

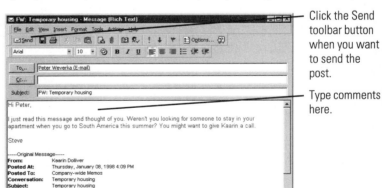

Click the Send toolbar button when you want to send the post.

Type comments here.

Printing a Post

You can print a post in the same way you print other Outlook items. First display the post. Then click the Print toolbar button.

If you want more control over how your post is printed, you can also choose the File menu's Print command. When Outlook displays the Print dialog box, choose a printer, specify the number of printed copies, describe what Outlook should do about any **attachments,** and so forth.

Preview Pane

Outlook shows a Preview pane when you're viewing your Inbox folder. The Preview pane shows a portion of the selected message item.

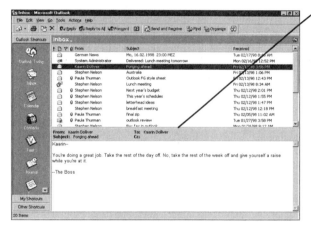

To change the sizes of the Folder List pane and the Preview pane, drag this bar.

SEE ALSO   AutoPreview

Priority SEE Importance

Private Appointments and Tasks

You can mark an **appointment** or **task** as private either when you create the appointment or task or later on, after you've created it. Making an appointment or task "private" so that others don't know about it may seem sort of funny, until you remember that other **users** may be able to view your Calendar if you have given them **delegate access** permission. For example, you may not want your coworkers to know that you are visiting a doctor or that you are involved in a confidential meeting.

Select this check box to make an appointment private.

After you've marked a task or appointment as private, your co-workers can't see its details, even if they have **permission** to view your **Calendar** and Tasks list.

Viewing Other Outlook Users' Calendars

If you want to know what your coworkers' schedules look like, you must get delegate access to view their Calendars. Once you've done so, choose the File menu's Open command and the Open submenu's Other User's Folder command. Click Name, and select a name in the list in the Select Names dialog box. Click OK. Then select Calendar in the Folder drop-down list box, and click OK again. Outlook displays the Calendar of the person whose name you indicated.

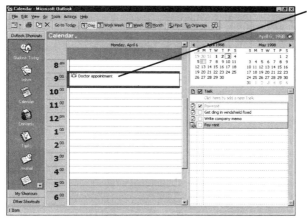

This is what an appointment looks like to you and other **network** users *before* you select the Private check box.

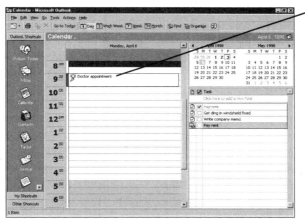

This is what an appointment looks like to you *after* you select the Private check box.

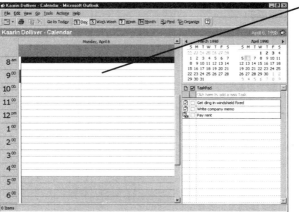

This is what an appointment looks like to other network users *after* you select the Private check box.

continues

Private Appointments and Tasks *(continued)*

Private text in your own schedule isn't hidden from you

The private text in your own Calendar and Tasks list isn't hidden from you. If you select an appointment or task, Outlook displays the appointment or task description.

Private Folder SEE Personal Folder

Profile

A profile lists the **information services** that an **e-mail client** such as Outlook knows how to use. You typically don't need to worry about or fiddle with profiles, however. The Outlook Setup program creates a profile for you when it installs the Outlook program by looking at the information services that you or your organization's **administrator** has already installed on your computer.

Program

In this book, I use the term *program* to refer to software applications such as Outlook. I should confess that this is slightly kooky because technical types call these things "applications." My thought, however, is that any piece of software that you start by making a choice from the Programs menu in Windows 95 or using the Program Manager in Windows 3.*x* is, in fact, a program.

Program Window

In this book, the term *program window* refers to the window that appears when you start **programs.** Calling them program windows is not entirely kosher, however. Traditionally, these windows have been called application windows. But I think program window is a better term because Windows (and most nontechnical people) refer to software products such as Outlook as programs. So it's really cleaner to call the windows these programs display program windows. At least that's what I think.

Public Folder

Public Folders are the folders where you store **posts** and files that you want to make available to lots of people. Typically, you store posts in a Public Folder so you don't have to waste time sending a bunch of people the same e-mail **message**.

Read and Unread Messages

Both read and unread **messages** can be found in the **Inbox** or any other message folder (if you move them there or set up rules so that they go there instead of into the Inbox). To help you know which is which, Outlook displays unread message information in boldface characters and read message information in regular characters. Take a look at the following figure to see what I mean.

I haven't read these messages.

I have read these messages.

By the way, the Edit menu provides several commands for marking and unmarking read and unread messages. To use one of these commands, simply select the message you want to mark or unmark and then choose the command.

SEE ALSO   Quick Reference: Edit Menu Commands

Read Receipt

Do you work with people who mysteriously lose or never receive the e-mail **messages** you send them? You know what I mean. You're in some really important meeting with the Big Cheese, and you say something like, "Well, I did send Geoffrey an e-mail message about all this..." And Geoffrey, who always was a bit slippery, says to the Big Cheese, "Hey, I *never* got that message."

Read receipts are made for such occasions. While a **delivery receipt** confirms that a message got to a user's **Mailbox,** a read receipt confirms that a **user** has actually opened the message. You can use read receipts if your computer is connected to a network. To ask the **Exchange server** to confirm that a message has been opened, click the Options toolbar button in the Message form and then select the Tell Me When This Message Has Been Read check box under Voting And Tracking Options.

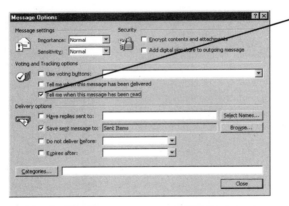

Select the Tell Me When This Message Has Been Read check box to ask the Exchange server to tell you when the message has been opened.

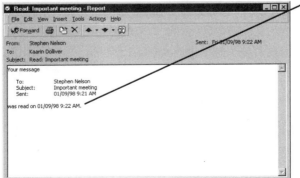

This is the type of message you receive, confirming that your message was opened.

A word of warning

Read receipts and delivery receipts appear to be the perfect tools in **organizations** where paranoia and backbiting run rampant. Unfortunately, however, they triple the workload of your server because every message you create can trigger the creation of two more messages from the server (the delivery receipt message and the read receipt message). And these extra messages slow down the system for everybody. I'm not going to tell you how to run your department. But I will say that there are probably better ways to deal with the Geoffreys of the world.

Recipient

A recipient is any person who receives an e-mail message, whether it is a forwarded message, a reply, a meeting request, or otherwise.

SEE ALSO   Sender

Recurring Appointment

You can create what's called a recurring appointment. In effect, this is an **appointment** that you want Outlook to schedule at a recurring interval: every day at 11:00 AM, every Friday at 5:00 PM, and so on. To create a recurring appointment, display the **Calendar** folder and then choose the Actions menu's New Recurring Appointment command. When Outlook displays the Appointment Recurrence dialog box, describe the appointment and how often it recurs.

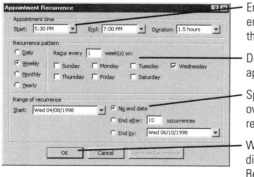

Enter the start time and end time or duration of the appointment.

Describe how often the appointment recurs.

Specify the range of time over which the appointment recurs.

When you click OK, Outlook displays the Untitled— Recurring Appointment dialog box.

continues

Recurring Appointment *(continued)*

Click the Save And Close toolbar button to record the appointment in your Calendar.

Describe the subject and location of the meeting.

Making an existing appointment recurring

If you want to make an existing appointment a recurring appointment, double-click the appointment to display its Appointment dialog box. Then click the Recurrence toolbar button and use the Appointment Recurrence dialog box to describe how often the appointment recurs.

SEE ALSO   Recurring Task

Recurring Task

You can tell Outlook to place a recurring **task** on your Tasks list. For example, if you prepare a report every Friday afternoon, you can add the "Do report" task to every Friday's Tasks list.

To create a recurring task, display your Tasks folder and click the New Task toolbar button. When Outlook displays the Task dialog box, use its boxes, buttons, and tabs to describe the task.

Name the task.

Specify a due date and start date for the task.

Set a **Reminder,** if needed.

Describe the task in more detail here.

When you finish describing the task using the Task dialog box, click the Recurrence toolbar button. Outlook displays the Task Recurrence dialog box.

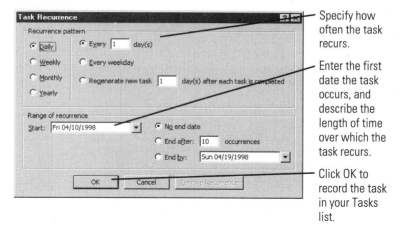

Specify how often the task recurs.

Enter the first date the task occurs, and describe the length of time over which the task recurs.

Click OK to record the task in your Tasks list.

Making an existing task recurring

If you want to make an existing task recurring, double-click it to display its Task dialog box. When you click the Recurrence toolbar button, Outlook displays the Task Recurrence dialog box. You can use it to describe how often the task recurs.

SEE ALSO   Recurring Appointment

Reminder

My grandmother, who is in her late eighties, has a system for re-membering things. She writes herself a note and puts it in a coffee can on her nightstand. As long as she regularly reviews the contents of the coffee can, she gets to her appointments on time. Outlook has a reminder system too—and it probably works better than my grandma's. (Grandma, after all, needs to remember to sift through the contents of her coffee can.) If you want to be reminded about an upcoming **task** or **appointment**, double-click the task or ap-pointment and then select the Reminder check box in the dialog box. Outlook identifies the appointments and tasks it will remind you about with a little bell icon.

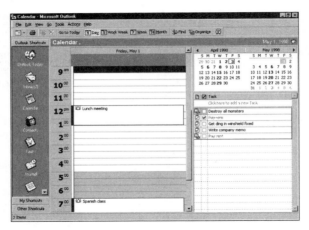

Ask not for whom the bell tolls. It tolls for thee.

SEE ALSO   Outlook Today

Remote Mail

Remote Mail is a useful tool for retrieving your e-mail while you're out of town and using another computer. Remote Mail lets you download only message headers and then choose from the headers which **messages** you want to download and read in their entirety. This can save you time and money if the computer you use on the road has a slower modem or if you must use a pay phone or make a long-distance connection. Remote Mail also lets you download cop-ies of the messages you receive while you're away and leave the original messages on the server. This means that when you return to the office, you can download the messages again to have copies of them in your Inbox at work. You don't need to go through the tedious process of copying the messages from the computer you used on the road to your desktop at work. To use Remote Mail, you must first set up Remote Mail on the computer you use on the road. This means making sure you have a Personal Folder file and Address Book on your computer, making sure that you have designated the Personal Folder file as a delivery location for your messages, and setting up your delivery service for use with Remote Mail. Once you have done this, you can use Remote Mail by choosing the Tools menu's Remote Mail command and then choosing a command from the Remote Mail submenu.

Using offline folders

If your network uses Microsoft Exchange Server, you have the option of using **offline folders** instead of, or in addition to, Remote Mail to make a remote connection. Offline folders give you several advantages over Remote Mail, including the ability to work with all of your Outlook folders, not just the Inbox.

SEE ALSO   **Synchronize**

Reply

You can respond to a **message** you receive with a new, or reply, message. To do this, select or display the message to which you want to respond and then click either the Reply or the Reply To All toolbar button. The Reply button addresses your reply to only the message sender. The Reply To All button addresses your reply to any other message recipients as well as the sender. Outlook opens the **Message form,** which you use to create your response.

Rules and Actions

The **Rules Wizard** and the **Out Of Office Assistant** use rules and actions to monitor and process incoming **messages.** For example, you might create a rule that tells Outlook to look for messages from your boss, and then you might specify an action for Outlook to take when it finds a message, such as to play a special sound.

R

Rules Wizard

The Rules Wizard helps you set rules that determine actions that
Outlook will take automatically when certain conditions are met.
For example, you can use the Rules Wizard to define an "important
message" and then tell Outlook to notify you when an important
message arrives by displaying a special pop-up announcement.

Using the Rules Wizard to Create a New Rule

To use the Rules Wizard to create a new rule, choose the Tools menu's Rules
Wizard command. When Outlook displays the first Rules Wizard dialog box, click
New. Then follow these steps:

1 In the first Rules Wizard
dialog box, select the
type of rule you want to
create in the Which Type
Of Rule Do You Want To
Create list box. Then
click Next.

2 In the second Rules Wizard dialog box, select the
condition(s) you want
Outlook to watch for.
Then click Next.

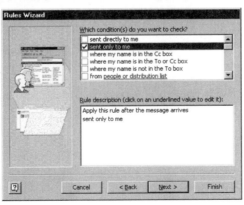

3 In the third Rules Wizard
dialog box, select the actions you want Outlook
to take when the
condition(s) you set are
met. Then click Next.

4 In the fourth Rules Wizard dialog box, select any exceptions to the rule. Then click Next.

5 In the final Rules Wizard dialog box, name the rule, select the Turn On This Rule check box, and click Finish.

Customizing rules

In any of the Rules Wizard dialog boxes, just click on any underlined text in the Rule Description box to customize that text. For example, click the underlined words in "sent to people or distribution list " and change them to "John Doe." (When you select an item containing underlined text in the upper text box, you can edit the text.)

Using the Rules Wizard to Apply an Existing Rule

After you've created a rule, you can apply (or disable) any rule by choosing the Tools menu's Rules Wizard command. When Outlook displays the first Rules Wizard dialog box, apply or disable rules by selecting or clearing check boxes. To change the order in which rules are applied, click Move Up or Move Down.

Click here to create a new rule.

Click here to edit an existing rule.

Click here to delete an existing rule.

SEE ALSO   Out Of Office Assistant; Rules and Actions

Schedule+ SEE **Microsoft Schedule+**

Sealed Message

As long as the **Exchange server** is configured the right way and Advanced Security is set up on the sender's and the recipient's Outlook clients, you can seal a **message** you've sent over a local area network. If you've signed up for a **digital ID** with a third-party verification service, you can also seal messages you send over the Internet.

SEE ALSO Encryption; Security

Second Time Zone

As an author, I often work with editors and publishers in other time zones. It is difficult to schedule **appointment** times with these people. You might think I could just add or subtract hours from my time, but that doesn't work. Some locations observe daylight saving time; others don't. And then, at least for me, things get really tricky when I'm working with someone on the other side of the International Date Line.

How a Second Time Zone Helps

Thankfully, Outlook provides a feature for straightening out these time considerations: you can add a second time zone's information to your daily **Calendar**. In this way, it's easy to describe an appointment by using times either in your time zone or that of the person with whom you are communicating.

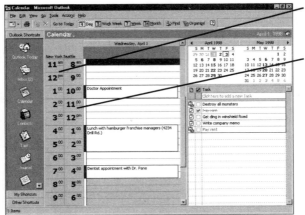

The first time zone's information.

The second time zone's information.

Adding a Second Time Zone

To add a second time zone, choose the Tools menu's Options command, click the Preferences tab, click Calendar Options, and then click Time Zone. Select the Show An Additional Time Zone check box to add a second set of appointment times to your daily Calendar. To describe the second time zone, use the buttons and boxes of the Time Zone dialog box.

Give the second time zone a label.

Select the second time zone.

Select this check box to automatically adjust for daylight saving time.

Security

Outlook provides different tools to make **e-mail** communications more secure. You can, for example, add digitally signed **messages** so that **recipients** and readers can be sure who messages came from and be sure as well that messages weren't tampered with. You can also encrypt messages so that they can't be read by recipients who don't know the **encryption** code.

To use any of these security tools on a network that includes an **Exchange server,** the security features must be installed on the **server** and enabled for the sender's **client** and all the recipients' clients. To use any of these security tools for Internet mail, you need to have a **digital ID.**

Security Zones

You can designate a security zone for incoming HTML messages to tell Outlook how much protection you want from running scripts in HTML messages that could damage files on your computer. Outlook's initial security zone settings already provide a high level of security, so you probably don't want to adjust the settings unless you first learn more about how security zones work (such as by reading the online documentation). To designate a security zone for incoming HTML messages, choose the Tools menu's Options command, click the Security tab, and then select a zone in the Zone drop-down list box. If you want to change the level of trust for the zone you choose, click Zone Settings. Note that if you change a zone's settings, the new settings apply to Microsoft Internet Explorer as well.

Sender

The sender is the person who creates and distributes a **message**. If I jot off a quick message to you suggesting lunch next Friday, for example, I'm the sender. You are the **recipient**.

Sensitivity

You can assign different levels of sensitivity to **messages.** By doing so, **recipients** can tell whether they might want to be alone when they read the message. To assign a sensitivity level to a message, click the Options toolbar button in the **Message form.** Then use the Sensitivity drop-down list box to select a sensitivity level: Normal, Personal, Private, or Confidential.

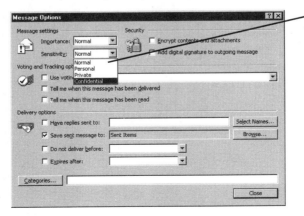

Message sensitivity information appears in the Sensitivity column of the **information viewer,** if that column is displayed.

How sensitivity affects messages

For the most part, message sensitivity doesn't affect anything. All it does is help recipients tell what kind of messages they've been sent. However, the Private sensitivity level is slightly different from the other three in that private messages, when they are forwarded or replied to, can't be edited. In other words, if you mark a message as private, the recipient can still **forward** it or **reply** to it. But Outlook doesn't let the recipient change the private message when he or she forwards or replies to it.

Server

In most **networks,** there are two kinds of computers: **clients** and servers. A client is what sits on top of or alongside people's desks. A server is what sits in the computer room or over in the corner of the office. The relationship between a client and a server is very much like the relationship between a diner and a waiter. The diner continually bugs the waiter with requests: "Cheese omelet," "More coffee," "Check please." On a computer network, the requests made by the client to the server are a little bit different: "Save this file," "Print this report," "Distribute these e-mail messages." But the process is very similar in both situations. The server's job is to quickly and efficiently respond to all of the questions and requests from each of the clients being served.

If your computer is part of a network, much of the software you use has both a client and a server component. Take, for example, the case of Outlook. The windows, **forms,** and dialog boxes that you see on your computer screen are displayed and controlled by the **Outlook client,** which is the software **program** running on your computer. The program that does the dirty work of passing **messages** around the network is actually Microsoft **Exchange Server,** which is the software program running on the server computer.

Service SEE Information Service

Setup Wizard

When you install the Outlook client, the installation program runs the Setup Wizard to create your **profile.** The profile, in essence, lists which information services you will use with Outlook and describes how Outlook connects to these **information services.**

Shortcut Icons

In general, shortcut icons on the **Outlook Bar** are divided into three groups: Outlook Shortcuts icons, My Shortcuts icons, and Other Shortcuts icons. The Outlook Shortcuts group includes shortcut icons that point to the standard Outlook folders, including the various Outlook **item** folders— **Inbox, Calendar, Contacts, Tasks, Journal,** and **Notes,** along with Deleted Items. The My Shortcuts icons point to a handful of special folders for dealing with Outlook's e-mail functions, including **Drafts,** Outbox, and Sent Items. The Other Shortcuts group provides icons that point to the My Computer folder, the My Documents folder, the **Favorites folder,** and any Public Folders you have on your network. Note that if you have upgraded from Outlook 97, however, your groups of shortcuts may be named Outlook, Mail, and Other. But these groups contain pretty much the same shortcut icons as the groups I have just described.

Smiley

As a means of communication, **e-mail** has certain drawbacks. Even with really good writers (so I hear), it's easy for comments to be misinterpreted and for nuances to be lost. For these reasons, a lot of people use what are called smileys in their **messages.** A smiley is a combination of punctuation characters that, taken together, form a smiley face, a frowning face, or another kind of face.

You'll see smileys in your correspondence, so I'm not going to provide examples of them here. (They don't look all that great in books like this anyway.) Before I close this little digression, however, I want to mention what happens to smileys when you enter them with **Microsoft Word.** If Word is your e-mail editor—and there's a good chance it is—Word takes the smiley faces and frowning faces that you build with punctuation marks and replaces them with equivalent characters from the Wingdings dingbat font. (A dingbat font is just a font with a bunch of crazy characters.)

 One of Smiley's people.

 Not one of Smiley's people.

SMTP

SMTP is the acronym for Simple Mail Transfer Protocol. SMTP is the set of rules and conventions that Outlook uses to pass e-mail **messages** to the **Internet.** You see this acronym used a few places in Outlook, but you don't really need to know anything about it.

Sorting

You can sort items in any Outlook **folder.** For example, Outlook lists **messages** in your **information viewer** in the order in which they were sent. But you can sort messages in other ways, for instance, by sender name or by message subject. To do this, choose the View menu's Current View command and then choose the Current View submenu's Customize Current View command. When Outlook displays the View Summary dialog box, click Sort. To specify how you want messages sorted, select entries from the Sort Items By and Then By boxes and then click the Ascending or Descending option buttons.

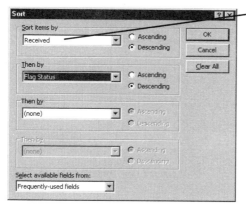

Specify how you want messages arranged in the Sort Items By drop-down list box.

Spam

Spam refers to **junk e-mail.** While spam may seem innocuous at first blush, it actually represents a big problem. Let me explain. What happens with spam is that somebody who wants to sell something—lets say it's investment advice—builds a list of thousands and thousands of **e-mail addresses.** (Special spam mailing programs can do this by looking at the e-mail names and addresses of the people who post messages to newsgroups and by looking at online directories of e-mail names and addresses.) Once the spammer has this list, he or she begins sending huge volleys of junk e-mail messages to the names on the mailing list. The spammer may also sell the mailing list to other spammers. So quite shortly thousands and thousands of spammers are all sending thousands and thousands of junk e-mail messages. This affects you personally in at least two ways. First, you may find your **Inbox** littered with junk e-mail messages (which causes all the same problems that junk snail-mail causes). Second, the high volume of spam that's being passed around the Internet (on some mail **servers** spam accounts for 80 to 90 percent of the message volume) means that spam wastes bandwidth. When spammers fill up the bandwidth, all the rest of us have to take longer to send or receive messages or wait longer for Web pages to download.

> **SEE ALSO** Flame; Junk E-Mail

Speed Dial

Speed Dial lets you create a list of phone numbers that you frequently call and then dial those numbers using your computer. (To use Speed Dial, you need to use the same telephone line for your modem and telephone.)

Adding Numbers to the Speed Dial Menu

To add numbers to the Speed Dial menu, display the Contacts folder, choose the Actions menu's Call Contact command, and then choose the Call Contact submenu's New Call command. When Outlook displays the New Call dialog box, click Dialing Options to display the Dialing Options dialog box.

Type the name of the person you want to add to the Speed Dial list.

Type the phone number of the person you want to add to the Speed Dial list.

Click Add and OK.

Using Speed Dial to Place a Call

To dial a number on the Speed Dial list, choose the Actions menu's Call Contact command and then choose the Call Contact submenu's Speed Dial command. Choose the number you want to call from the Speed Dial submenu. In the New Call dialog box, click Start Call and then pick up the receiver after your computer and modem finish dialing the number.

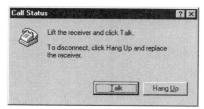

When Outlook displays the Call Status dialog box, click Talk. When you complete your call, click Hang Up, replace the receiver, and click End Call in the Dial Phone dialog box. Then select another number in the Dial Number drop-down list, or if you have no other calls to make, click Close.

Spelling Checker

You can—and you should—use Outlook's spelling checker to correct spelling errors in your e-mail **messages.** Misspelled words in messages make a bad impression. To check the spelling of the words in a message, choose the Tools menu's Spelling command. If Outlook finds a misspelled word, it displays the Spelling dialog box.

continues

Spelling Checker *(continued)*

Outlook shows the misspelled word here.

Make your correction here.

Select a suggestion by clicking it.

Spelling Buttons

The buttons in the Spelling dialog box assist in spell-checking and error-correction.

Button	What it does
Ignore	Ignores only this occurrence of the word.
Ignore All	Ignores this and every other occurrence of the word.
Change	Changes this occurrence of the word to what the Change To box shows.
Change All	Changes this and every other occurrence of the word to what the Change To box shows.
Add	Adds the word to the spelling dictionary.
Suggest	Looks for similarly spelled words in the spelling dictionary.

Spelling Options

You can control, to a minor extent, the way in which Outlook's spelling checker works. To do this, choose the Tools menu's Options command and click the Spelling Tab. Or with the Spelling dialog box on your screen, click Options.

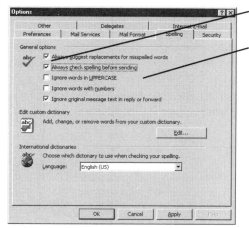

I recommend selecting both of these check boxes.

The Ignore options (the last three) let you weed out word and character strings that aren't going to appear in any dictionary—such as proper nouns, acronyms, and alphanumeric codes. You can also tell Outlook to ignore the original text.

SEE ALSO   Check Names

Status Bar

The status bar appears along the bottom edge of the Outlook **program window** and tells you how many **items** are in the **folder** you selected. (If you don't see the status bar, choose the View menu's Status Bar command.)

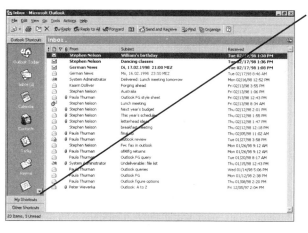

The Outlook status bar counts the items in the selected folder.

Subfolder

A subfolder is a folder within a folder. Using subfolders is a good way to organize your messages.

Subject

When you create a **message,** you have the option of including a brief description of the message's subject. I recommend including meaningful subject descriptions with messages. They make it easier for people to **sort** and **filter** messages. By including a subject, you increase the chances of someone saving your message for future reference. And **recipients** will probably read your messages sooner.

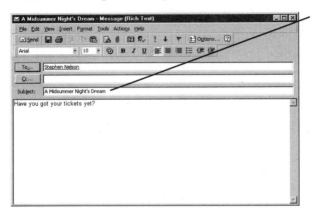

Here's where you enter the message subject. As soon as you do, Outlook renames the **Message form** using the subject.

Synchronize

If you work with **offline folders,** you need to synchronize your online and offline folders when you log on to your network. When you synchronize your folders, any changes you make while using your folders offline are incorporated into your online folders so that sets of folders are identical. To synchronize folders, choose the Tools menu's Synchronize command and then choose the Synchronize submenu's All Folders command.

SEE ALSO   Remote Mail

Task Filters

Outlook lets you filter the tasks in the **Tasks** list so you can decide which tasks appear in the list. For example, you can show only tasks that you haven't yet finished, or tasks that you should have finished by now but haven't, or even tasks that you haven't yet started. To perform this filtering, choose the View menu's Current View command and then choose the Current View submenu's Customize Current View command. When Outlook displays the View Summary dialog box, click Filter.

SEE ALSO   Folder View

Task List SEE Tasks

TaskPad

The TaskPad is the small task list you see in the lower right corner of the **Calendar** folder. When you add a new task to the TaskPad, it shows up on the main Tasks list in the **Tasks** folder.

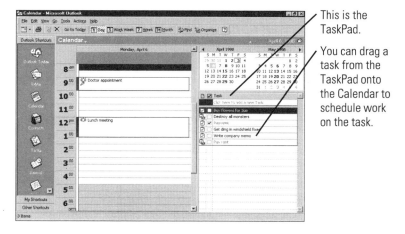

This is the TaskPad.

You can drag a task from the TaskPad onto the Calendar to schedule work on the task.

Tasks

Outlook lets you build a list of the tasks you're supposed to do. You can organize tasks into projects by grouping them into **categories,** or you can **group** them by a variety of other criteria. You can **filter** tasks to display certain ones, **sort** tasks in the Tasks list, and drag tasks to move them up and down in the Tasks list. You can even assign tasks to your coworkers, track the progress you've made on completing tasks, and send reports to your colleagues describing the **task status.**

continues

Tasks *(continued)*

Adding a Task to the Tasks List

To add a task to your Tasks list, click the Tasks icon on the **Outlook Bar.** Then click the top line of the Tasks list in the Subject **field** (where it says *Click here to add a new Task*).

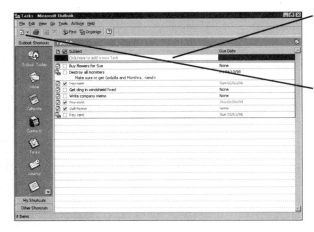

Type a short description of the task.

Alternatively, to provide more detailed information about a task you're adding, click the New Task toolbar button. Outlook displays the Untitled— Task window.

Use the tabs, buttons, and boxes in the Task window to describe the task in detail.

Viewing the Tasks List

Outlook supplies ten predefined **views** of the Tasks list, including Simple List, Detailed List, Active Tasks, Completed Tasks, and Task Timeline. To select which tasks appear, choose the View menu's Current View command.

Assigning a Task

If you have the authority, you can assign tasks to your coworkers using Outlook. Double-click an existing task on the Tasks list, or click the New Task toolbar button to open a new Task form. In the Task form, click the Assign Task toolbar button. Outlook displays an altered Task form.

Click the Send toolbar button to assign the task.

To assign the task, click To.

Select these check boxes to stay informed on the status of the task.

The person to whom you assign the task can accept, decline, or reassign the task request.

Accepting, Declining, and Reassigning Tasks

If you are assigned a task, you can accept it by clicking Accept. When Outlook displays the Accepting Task dialog box, you can simply accept the task or you can accept it and add a comment. To accept a task without adding a comment, click the Send The Response Now option button and then click OK. To add a comment, click the Edit The Response Before Sending option button and then click OK. Type your response, and then click Send. When you accept a task, you become the "owner" of the task.

To decline a task you have been assigned, click Decline. When Outlook displays the Declining A Task dialog box, you can decline the task or you can decline it and add a comment. To decline a task without adding a comment, click the Send The Response Now option button and then click OK. To add a comment, click the Edit The Response Before Sending option button and then click OK. Type your response, and then click Send. The task is returned to the person who sent it to you.

To reassign a task, open the message that contains the task request. Click Assign Task, and type the name of the person to whom you want to assign the task in the To box. Then click Send. The new task recipient then has the option of accepting, declining, or reassigning the task.

continues

Tasks *(continued)*

Categorizing and Prioritizing Tasks

To assign a task to a **category,** click Categories and select a category from the list in the Categories dialog box or create a new category. Then click OK.

To prioritize a task, display the Priority drop-down list and select Normal, High, or Low priority from the list. High-priority tasks are marked with a red exclamation point in the Detailed List Task view.

SEE ALSO   Recurring Task; Task Status

Task Status

You can track the status of a task you are working on and let other members of your workgroup know the task status. Tasks can be assigned the status Not Started, In Progress, Completed, Waiting On Someone Else, or Deferred. In addition, you can indicate the percent completion of a task and note the total and actual work done on a task.

Tracking the Status of a Task

To display a task in your Tasks list, double-click it or click the New Task button to open a new Task form. Click the Task tab, select a status from the Status drop-down list, and use the % Complete spin box to indicate the percentage of the task already completed. Then click the Details tab.

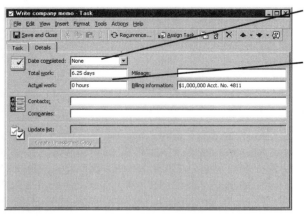

Enter the date the task was completed.

Describe the work done on the task.

Sending a Task Status Report

To send a task status report, right-click the task in the Tasks list. Choose the shortcut menu's Send Status Report command. Outlook displays the Task Status Report—Message form.

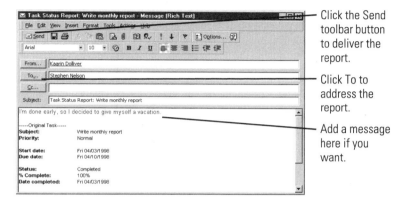

Click the Send toolbar button to deliver the report.

Click To to address the report.

Add a message here if you want.

Tentative Appointment

A tentative appointment shows up in your appointment **Calendar,** but it isn't considered **busy time.** As a result, an **appointment** that you mark as tentative doesn't preclude the **Plan A Meeting Wizard** from scheduling a meeting for the same time as the tentative appointment.

Thread SEE Conversation Thread

Time Zone SEE Second Time Zone

To-Do List

Outlook lets you keep an online to-do list, which it calls a **Tasks** list. With the list, you can keep track of the tasks you're supposed to do but haven't yet done. That report for your boss. The telephone call to the sales guys in Atlanta. A birthday present for your daughter.

SEE ALSO   Reminder; TaskPad

T

Toolbar

Outlook features toolbars to make things easier for you. (A toolbar is just a group of clickable buttons.) Because it's usually easier to click a button than choose a command, I emphasize the toolbar way in this little book. Like all the other programs in Microsoft Office, Outlook has menus that display toolbar-button icons next to menu commands to help you remember the association. By the way, if your **program window** doesn't show a toolbar, choose the View menu's Toolbars command, and then choose one of the toolbars listed.

Customize a Toolbar

Outlook 98 lets you customize your toolbars and create your own custom toolbars. To customize an existing toolbar, right-click the toolbar and choose the shortcut menu's Customize command. This displays the Customize dialog box. Use the Commands tab of this dialog box to drag menu commands to the toolbar. To edit a toolbar button, display the Customize dialog box and then right-click the toolbar button. Use the shortcut menu to rename the button or change its options. To rearrange the buttons on a toolbar, display the Customize dialog box and then drag the buttons to new locations on the toolbar. To create a new toolbar, click New in the Customize dialog box.

SEE ALSO   Quick Reference: Toolbar Buttons

Undo

You can typically undo your last editing change to a **message.** To do this, choose the Edit menu's Undo command.

Unread Messages SEE Read and Unread Messages

URL

The URL, short for Uniform Resource Locator, specifies how you find an **Internet** resource such as a **World Wide Web** page. A URL has four parts: the service, or protocol; the server name; the path; and the document, or file, name.

A Sample URL Explained

Let me explain the four parts of a URL by using a real-life **Web page**—the cover page of the Internal Revenue Service's online newspaper called the *Digital Daily.* Here it is:

http://www.irs.ustreas.gov/prod/cover.html

http:// identifies this resource as part of the World Wide Web

www.irs.ustreas.gov/ identifies the server

prod/ names the directory of the World Wide Web document

cover.html names the World Wide Web document

SEE ALSO   HTML; Hyperlink

Users

Users are the people who use Outlook. (In particular, they're the ones who use it as a network **client**.) Regular folk like you and me.

SEE ALSO   Administrator

Uuencode

Some e-mail systems (although thankfully not Outlook) don't let you include files in your e-mail **message.** With these systems, you can send only text.

Okay. I know what you're thinking. Not being able to attach a nontext file to an e-mail message seems like a pretty big limitation. And you're right. So to deal with this limitation, people created a **program** called Uuencode (pronounced you-you-en-code). It converts, or encodes, nontext files to text files so that they can be included in e-mail messages such as those sent over the Internet. At the other end, when the **recipient** gets the message, the program converts, or decodes, the text files and turns them back into nontext files.

continues

Uuencode *(continued)*

This is a uuencoded attachment.

You now know more than you need to about Uuencode. Outlook takes care of encoding and decoding Internet e-mail **attachments** automatically. And unless you specify that you want to use Uuencode, Outlook uses something called **MIME** for e-mail attachments you send.

VCard

A vCard is a virtual business card you attach to Internet e-mail messages. You can exchange vCards in e-mail messages as a quick and easy way of distributing your contact information. When you receive a vCard from someone, you can save the vCard as a contact item. To create a vCard, display the **Contacts** folder, right-click the contact for whom you want to create a vCard, and then choose the shortcut menu's Export To VCard File command. When Outlook displays the Save As dialog box, make sure the Save As Type box says VCARD files. To save a vCard that someone sends you, double-click the vCard attachment (so that Outlook opens the Contacts dialog box), enter any additional information you want to record, and then click Save And Record.

Views

Each Outlook **folder** comes with several different views. A view organizes the **items** in a folder by specifying which **fields** appear, how items should be **grouped** or **sorted,** and whether any **filters** should be used. Outlook offers many types of views. Some view types are better suited for particular Outlook items.

Choosing a View

To select a view, choose the View menu's Current View command. When Outlook displays the Current View submenu, select the view you want to use. Note that different Outlook folders offer different views.

Modifying a Standard View

You can modify standard Outlook views to suit your preferences and needs. To do so, display a standard view, choose the View menu's Current View command, and then choose the Current View submenu's Customize Current View command. When Outlook displays the View Summary dialog box, click a button to tell Outlook how you want to modify the view.

Click Fields to change the fields displayed in the view.

Click Group By to change the grouping of items in the view.

Click Sort to change the way items in the view are sorted.

Click Filter to change which items are included in the view.

Click Other Settings to change fonts, column headings, and other aspects of the way items in the view are formatted.

Defining a New View

The standard views that Outlook initially provides may be the only ones you need. But you can easily create your own views. Choose the View menu's Current View command, and then choose the Current View submenu's Define Views command. When Outlook displays the Define Views dialog box, click New. Outlook displays the Create A New View dialog box.

continues

Views *(continued)*

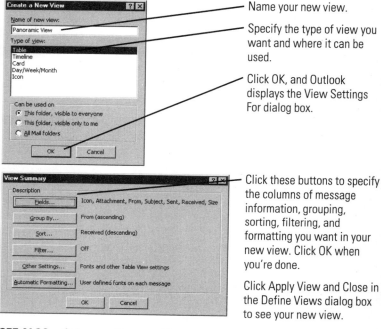

Name your new view.

Specify the type of view you want and where it can be used.

Click OK, and Outlook displays the View Settings For dialog box.

Click these buttons to specify the columns of message information, grouping, sorting, filtering, and formatting you want in your new view. Click OK when you're done.

Click Apply View and Close in the Define Views dialog box to see your new view.

SEE ALSO   Columns; Message Flag

Voting Buttons

You can put voting buttons on e-mail messages so that recipients can reply merely by clicking "Yes" or "No"; "Accept" or "Reject"; or "Yes," "No," or "Maybe." To create a democratic message, fill in the Message form and click the Options toolbar button. Then select the Use Voting Buttons check box, and select a set of voting buttons.

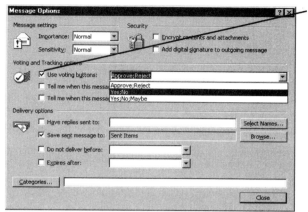

Select this check box to add voting buttons to a message, and then select a set of voting buttons.

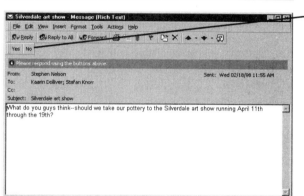

Here's how voting buttons look on a Message form.

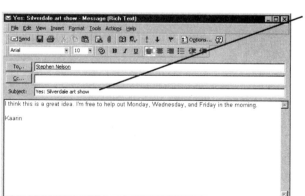

Here's what a reply message looks like.

Web Browser

A Web browser is a program that lets you look at World Wide Web documents. Netscape Navigator and NCSA Mosaic are browsers, as is Microsoft Internet Explorer (which comes with Outlook 98). Most browsers let you browse, or view, both the graphics and text components of World Wide Web documents, but there are also browsers that let you look at just the text. (You might want to do this, for example, if your connection to the Internet is slow—say, less than 28.8 Kbps—or if you really are interested in only the text portions of the documents you are viewing.)

SEE ALSO Web Page

Web Page

Web page is another name for a document on the **World Wide Web,** the most popular part of the **Internet.** Web pages often combine text, graphics, and other elements, including sound and movie or video clips. Web pages also usually include **hyperlinks,** or jumps, to other Web pages.

Word SEE Microsoft Word

Word Mail Merge

You can use the name and address information stored in your Outlook Contacts folder in a Microsoft Word mail merge. For information about how to do this, refer to your Word documentation.

World Wide Web

The World Wide Web (also known as WWW or simply the Web) is a set of multimedia documents that are connected so you can jump from one document to another using **hyperlinks,** usually with just a click. The multimedia part means that you're not limited to words: you can place pictures, sounds, and even video clips in a Web document.

Outlook A to Z

Z

To view a WWW document, you need to have a **Web browser.**
Popular Web browsers include Netscape Navigator, NCSA Mosaic,
and Microsoft Internet Explorer. If you want to start exploring the
Web, try using a search tool such as Yahoo! You can find it at the
following URL:

http://www.yahoo.com.

It provides a directory of thousands of different World Wide Web
sites.

ZIP

I figured since this part of the book is called Outlook A to Z, I
needed at least one "Z" entry. So let me tell you about ZIP. ZIP
actually refers to a data-compression technique. When people say
a **file** is zipped, they usually mean it's been compressed using the
PKZIP or WinZip utility. To use a zipped file, you have to unzip it.
If a file has been zipped with PKZIP, for example, you have to unzip
it with PKUNZIP.

Zipping a large file before you attach it to an e-mail message is
a good idea—especially if you have the problems of limited disk
space or slow transmission times. Ask your **administrator** for
more information.

Troubleshooting

Got a problem? Starting on
the next page are solutions
to the problems that sometimes plague new users of
Microsoft Outlook 98. You'll
be on your way—and safely
out of trouble—in no time.

E-Mail

You Don't Know Someone's E-Mail Address

You want to send so-and-so an e-mail **message,** but you don't have the address? Don't feel embarrassed. I think this is probably the most common e-mail problem of all. Really. Fortunately, this problem is easy to solve.

 Check the Global Address List

If the certain someone to whom you want to send a message is an Outlook **user** on the same **network,** you can get the **e-mail name** from the **Global Address List.** To do this, click the Address Book toolbar button and follow these steps:

1 Select Global Address List from the Show Names From The list box.

2 Scroll through the list of names until you find the person to whom you want to send a message.

 Call them and ask

If someone isn't a user on your network but your Outlook system is connected to the **Internet,** you can still send the message. You just can't look up the missing address in your Global Address List. Your best bet is to call and ask for the correct e-mail name. Sounds silly, doesn't it? But this really is the best solution. So go and do it. You need to get both the person's e-mail name and the domain name. Once you know this information, you just send your message to

e-mailname@domainname

For example, if you wanted to send an e-mail message to me at my Microsoft Network address, you would send the message to:

`stphnlnlsn@msn.com`

stphnlnlsn is my Microsoft Network user name. And *msn.com* is the Microsoft Network domain name. If you're wondering where in the world I got my user name, it's just my first name, middle initial, and last name, without any vowels.

Ask them to e-mail you first

If you want to send someone e-mail but your real problem is that you're not familiar with this computerized, electronic mail thing, your best bet may be to get the other person to send you an e-mail message. (You may need to ask your **administrator** for your e-mail name and domain name if the other person will be sending you e-mail over the Internet.) But if you provide this information to the person with whom you want to correspond and he or she is technically astute, it will be easy for the other person to send e-mail to you.

When you get the message—you'll see it in your **Inbox**—double-click it and read it. Then right-click the sender's name in the **message header,** and choose the Add To Personal Address Book command or Add To Contacts command when Outlook displays the shortcut menu. What you've just done is added the sender's e-mail name (and all the other information you need to send him or her e-mail messages) to your **Personal Address Book** or **Contacts** list.

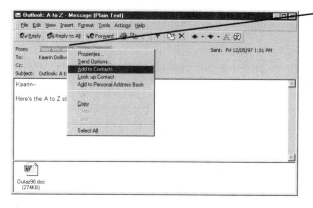

Right-click here to display the shortcut menu.

continues

You Don't Know Someone's E-Mail Address *(continued)*

After you've added a person's name to your Personal Address Book or Contacts list, it's easy to address a message to the person. All you have to do is click To or Cc when you're writing the message so that Outlook displays the Select Names dialog box. Then follow these steps:

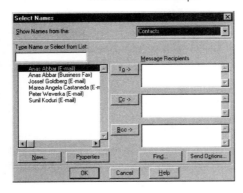

1 Select Personal Address Book or Contacts from the Show Names From The list box.

2 Scroll through the list of names until you find the person to whom you want to send a message.

3 Double-click the person's name.

 Search directories on the Web

If you want to find a long-lost friend's e-mail address, try conducting an online search using a directory service. To do this, click the Start button and choose the Find command. Then choose the Find menu's People command. Use the Look In drop-down list box to select the name of a directory service. (It doesn't really matter which one you choose first—you'll probably have to try several.) Then enter as much of the person's name as you can remember in the Name box, and click Find Now. The directory service lists all the names in its database that match the text you entered. If the directory service didn't find a match, don't give up. Try another service, or try adding more or less information to the Name text box.

Your Messages Aren't Getting Through

Occasionally, a message recipient might not receive a message you sent, even though you used the correct address. Here are a few ways you can help determine the cause of this problem and solve it.

E-mail yourself a message to make sure the Exchange server is running

Your first step should be to e-mail yourself a message. You can do this simply by naming yourself in the message as the recipient. The **Outlook client** delivers the message to the **Exchange server** and then, assuming everything goes smoothly, the Exchange server delivers the message to your **Inbox.**

If you can't e-mail yourself a message, by the way, contact the **administrator.** The problem isn't actually yours to worry about: it's the administrator's problem. (Do, however, make sure you are really e-mailing yourself and not somebody else with a similar name in another department.)

Request a return receipt or a read-notification receipt

If most of your messages reach their recipients but certain types don't seem to get through—or messages to certain recipients don't seem to get through—the problem might be one of human error. For example, Joe Bob in purchasing might have forgotten that he received messages from you. In cases like these, you can tell Outlook to alert you to the fact that, for example, Joe Bob has indeed received your message or that Joe Bob has indeed read your message. To do this, click the Options toolbar button when the **Message form** is displayed.

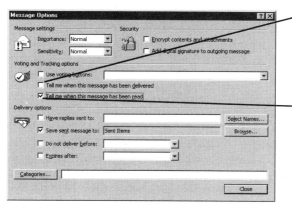

Select this tracking option to have the server acknowledge delivery of your message.

Select this tracking option to have the server monitor the recipient's Inbox and tell you when the recipient opened the message.

You're Getting Too Many Messages

In **organizations** where everybody uses e-mail, it's easy to get overwhelmed with e-mail **messages.** Secretaries. Managers with lots of direct and indirect subordinates. People in service departments. The truth is, short of an organizational e-mail policy that attempts to limit frivolous e-mail traffic, you can't do much to reduce the volume of incoming messages. But I do have three ideas for you if you're getting overloaded.

Don't use read receipts or delivery notifications wantonly

Okay, I know I said earlier that **read receipts** and **delivery receipts** are useful for dealing with the Joe Bobs of the world. But they also clog up your **Inbox** with one or two extra messages for every message you send. So don't use them unless you have to.

Don't needlessly reply to or forward messages

As sure as the sun rises in the east, the more messages you **reply** to and **forward,** the more you'll receive. The reason, of course, is that the recipient of a reply message or forwarded message generates another reply a certain percentage of the time. And this is true even if you shouldn't have created the reply message or forwarded the message in the first place.

I'm not suggesting that you stop replying to your boss's messages or that you not forward him or her messages when appropriate. But you should be judicious. It's easy to reply to or forward messages, but it isn't always necessary.

Use the Organize pane to filter messages

You can get Outlook's help when it comes to managing incoming messages. Just create a rule using the **Organize pane** or the **Rules Wizard** that tells Outlook to move certain messages to other folders or delete junk e-mail, as appropriate. To do this, click the Organize toolbar button in the Inbox.

Are you getting junk mail?

If you're getting electronic mail from someone you'd rather not correspond with, you can use the Organize pane to automatically delete all messages you receive from that person. To do this, click the Organize pane's Junk E-Mail tab. Use this tab to name the joker who keeps sending you e-mail, and tell Outlook to delete any messages he or she sends you.

Your Folders Are Full

Folders can quickly overflow with **messages** if you regularly correspond via e-mail. Fortunately, it's easy to clean up a folder.

Delete individual messages you don't need

To delete a message, select it and then click the Delete toolbar button. If you want to save a copy of a message, be sure to print it before you delete it.

Empty the Deleted Items folder

You can delete all the messages in your Deleted Items folder by right-clicking the Deleted Items folder and choosing the shortcut menu's Empty "Deleted Items" Folder command. It's a good idea to regularly remove the messages in the Deleted Items folder. (When you delete a message in the **Inbox,** Outbox, or Sent Items folders, Outlook moves the message to the Deleted Items folder, so it can fill up rather fast.)

Choose the Empty "Deleted Items" Folder command to remove items from the selected folder.

Calendar and Tasks

You Can't Schedule a Meeting

Outlook can be a marvelous tool for scheduling meetings, but scheduling can be a challenge when people are busy. Nevertheless, there are some things you can do to make it easier to schedule meetings.

Use tentative appointments

Perhaps the easiest thing to do is tell Outlook that the **appointments** you schedule are **tentative appointments.** This way, the appointment time-slots you set aside don't fall into the **busy time** category, and Outlook can use them to schedule meetings. To indicate that an appointment is tentative, double-click the appointment to display the Appointment dialog box.

Select Tentative in the Show Time As list box to designate the appointment as tentative.

Leave free time in your schedule

If you leave free time in your schedule—and everybody you work with does the same—you'll find it much easier to schedule meetings. You can even create a tentative appointment, perhaps called "meetings," and use it as an empty slot into which to plop real meetings. For real men and real women.

Schedule shorter meetings

What Outlook looks for when it schedules a meeting is a block of free time that is available to every meeting attendee. For this reason, it's easier to schedule half-hour meetings than to schedule one-hour meetings or two-hour meetings. There are many more half-hour slots in a day than there are one-hour or two-hour slots, after all.

You Want Your Calendar and Task List to Be Private

As you may know, almost everyone who uses Outlook can retrieve your free and busy time information from your **Calendar.** You may wonder, then, how private or public your schedule and **Tasks** list are. Unfortunately, I can't give you specific information about how private your schedule and Tasks list are, but I can give you some ideas for gaining a bit more privacy on the **network.**

▶

Ask your administrator about delegate access permissions

You or the network **administrator** set what are called **delegate access** permissions to your schedule. Delegate access permissions determine who can view your Outlook information and whether they can change it. The default setting, by the way, is for other **users** to be able to see only when you're busy and when you're not. It's possible, however, for people to see much more detail. It all depends on the delegate access permissions. To view the delegate access permissions for a folder, right-click the folder in the Outlook Bar and choose the shortcut menu's Properties command. Then click the Permissions tab. If you have permission from your administrator to do so, you may be able to edit the delegate access permissions here for the folder you selected.

One more thing: if people can view your daily or weekly Calendar, they can see appointment and Tasks list descriptions as well. You can, however, create private appointment and task descriptions.

SEE ALSO   Private Appointments and Tasks

Quick Reference

Any time you explore a new
program, you're bound to
see features and tools you
can't identify. To be sure
you can identify the
commands and toolbar
buttons you see in
Microsoft Outlook 98,
this Quick Reference
describes these items in
systematic detail.

Outlook Inbox Menu Commands

File Menu

New — Displays the New submenu of items you can create

Mail Message Opens a new Message form

Post In This Folder Displays the Post form so you can place a post (or a file) in a folder

Folder... Lets you create a new folder

Outlook Bar Shortcut... Lets you add a folder icon to the Outlook Bar

Appointment Opens a new Appointment form

Meeting Request Opens a new Meeting Request form

Contact Opens a new Contact form

Task Opens a new Task form

Task Request Opens a new Task Request form

Journal Entry Opens a new Journal Entry form

Note Opens a new Note

Office Document Opens a new Microsoft Office document

Choose Form... Opens a custom Outlook form

Personal Folders File (.pst)... Opens the Create Personal Folders dialog box

Open — Opens the selected folder so you can see its contents or the selected message so you can read it

Selected Items Opens a message, task, or other item

Other User's Folder... Opens a Personal Folder from another person on the network

Personal Folders File (.pst)... Opens a Personal folder

Close All Items — Closes all open Outlook items, including items minimized to the Taskbar

Save As... — Saves the selected message in a different folder

Save Attachments — Saves any attachments to the selected message in a different folder

Folder	Displays the Folder submenu
	New FolderFile... Creates a new subfolder in the selected folder
	Move... Moves the selected folder or message to a different location
	Copy... Copies the selected folder or message to a different location
	Copy Folder Design... Copies the permissions, rules, description, forms, and views of the open folder
	Delete Deletes the selected message or folder
	Rename... Renames the selected folder
	Add To Public Folder Favorites Adds the selected folder to the Favorites subfolder of Public Folders
	Remove From Public Folder Favorites Removes the selected folder from the Favorites subfolder of Public Folders
	Properties For Lets you view or change the Properties of the selected message or folder
Import And Export...	Invokes the Import And Export Wizard
Archive...	Displays the Archive dialog box, enabling you to create Archive files
Page Setup	Displays the Page Setup submenu
	Table Style Opens the Page Setup: Table Style dialog box to let you set table style printing options for printing messages
	Memo Style Opens the Page Setup: Memo Style dialog box to let you set memo style printing options for printing messages
	Define Print Styles... Opens the Define Print Styles dialog box
Print Preview	Displays a window that shows how printed messages look
Print...	Prints the selected message
Work Offline	Disconnects you if you are currently working online
Exit	Stops the Outlook client program
Exit And Log Off	Stops the Outlook client program and any other workgroup programs

Edit Menu

Undo	Reverses, or undoes, the last action
Cut	Moves the current folder or item to the Clipboard
Copy	Moves a copy of the current folder or item to the Clipboard
Paste	Copies the Clipboard contents to the current folder
Clear	Deletes the selected item(s)
Select All	Selects all the messages in the open folder
Delete	Deletes the selected item(s)
Move To Folder...	Moves the selected item(s) to the folder you select
Copy To Folder...	Copies the selected item(s) to the folder you select
Mark As Read	Marks the selected message as one you've already read
Mark As Unread	Marks the selected message as one you haven't yet read
Mark All As Read	Marks all of the messages in the open folder as ones you've read
Categories...	Lets you assign the selected item(s) to a category

View Menu

Current View	Lets you change the current view of the information viewer
Messages	Displays all messages
Messages With AutoPreview	Displays a short preview of unread messages
By Follow Up Flag	Groups messages by follow-up flag
Last Seven Days	Lists only messages from the past week
Flagged For Next Seven Days	Lists only messages that were flagged for the next week
By Conversation Topic	Groups messages by conversation topic
By Sender	Groups messages by sender
Unread Messages	Lists unread messages only
Sent To	Lists the time messages were sent and the names of the message recipients

Message Timeline   Displays messages along a timeline

Customize Current ViewFile... Displays the View Summary
dialog box so you can edit a view

Define Views...   Lets you create your own view

Outlook Bar Displays or hides the Outlook Bar of items and folders

Folder List Displays or hides the Folder List from the Outlook program
window (Outlook marks the command with a check mark when
the Folder List is present.)

Preview Pane Toggles the Preview pane on and off

AutoPreview Displays a short preview of each message

Expand/Collapse Groups Displays a submenu of commands for expanding and
collapsing groups if the view uses groups

Toolbars Displays the Toolbars submenu

Standard   Displays or hides the Standard toolbar

Advanced   Display or hides the Advanced toolbar

Remote   Displays or hides the Remote Mail toolbar

Customize... Displays a dialog box for rearranging the
buttons on the toolbars

Status Bar Displays or hides the Outlook program window's status bar
(Outlook marks the command with a check mark when the
status bar is present.)

Go Menu

Back Displays the previously selected folder

Forward Displays the folder that was selected when Back was clicked

Up One Level Displays the folder that contains the selected folder

Go To Folder... Moves to a folder elsewhere on your hard drive or network

Outlook Today Opens a window that lists Outlook items that need addressing

Inbox Displays your Inbox

Drafts Displays your Drafts folder

continues

Go Menu *(continued)*

Calendar	Displays your Calendar
Contacts	Displays your Contacts folder
Tasks	Displays your Tasks folder
News	Opens Outlook Express News
Web Browser	Starts your default Web browser
Internet Call	Displays the Internet Call submenu

> **From Address Book...** Displays a dialog box that allows you to place a NetMeeting call to a person in an Address Book List
>
> **Internet Call** Starts Microsoft NetMeeting

Tools Menu

Send	Sends outgoing e-mail messages
Send And Receive	Lets you choose the services to check for new e-mail
Synchronize	Displays the Synchronize submenu for synchronizing Exchange folders

> **All Folders** Updates all your offline folders so they match the server folders that Outlook uses for the actual delivery and storage of real messages
>
> **This Folder** Updates the selected offline folder so it matches its server folder
>
> **Download Address Book** Grabs the address lists from the Exchange server's Address Book and stores them in the Address Book on your hard disk

Remote Mail	Displays the Remote Mail submenu

> **Connect...** Dials your computer from a remote location so you can download message headers
>
> **Disconnect** Ends the dial-up connection to your computer from a remote location
>
> **Mark To Retrieve** Marks the messages you want to download to your computer when you reconnect

Mark To Retrieve A Copy   Marks the messages you want to download to your computer while leaving a copy on the server

Delete   Removes messages both from your computer and from the server

Unmark   Changes the status of a message that you had previously marked to download

Unmark All   Changes the status of all the messages that you had previously marked to download

Remote Tools   Displays the Remote toolbar

Address Book...   Displays the Address Book

Find   Lets you locate messages that match your description

Advanced Find...   Opens the Find dialog box with many options for finding items

Organize   Opens the Organize pane

Rules Wizard...   Starts the Rules Wizard, a tool for monitoring and managing incoming messages and other items

Out Of Office Assistant...   Starts the Out Of Office Assistant, a tool for automatically handling messages you receive when you are out of the office

Microsoft Fax Tools   Displays a submenu of commands for working with faxes and setting fax options

Empty "Deleted Items" Folder   Removes all the items from the Deleted Items folder

Recover Deleted Items...   Allows you to recover messages deleted from the Exchange server

Forms   Displays the Forms submenu

Choose Form...   Allows you to choose the form you want to use for creating an Outlook item

Design A Form...   Allows you to design a custom form for creating Outlook items

Accounts... / Services...   Describes and lets you change the information services available to the Outlook client

Options...   Displays a dialog box you can use to control how the Outlook client works

Actions Menu

New Mail Message	Displays the Message form so you can create a new message
New Fax Message	Opens a dialog box you can use to create a new fax
New Mail Message Using	Displays a submenu so you can choose how you want to compose the message
Flag For Follow Up...	Lets you flag a message so you can follow through with it later
Junk E-Mail	Displays the Junk E-Mail submenu
	Add To Junk Senders List Adds the sender of the selected message to your Junk Senders list
	Add To Adult Content Senders List Add the sender of the selected message to your Adult Content Senders list
Find All	Opens the Find All submenu
	Related Messages... Finds message with similar content and characteristics
	Messages From Sender... Finds other messages from the sender
Reply	Displays the RE: (Reply) form so you can respond to a message by sending the sender a new message
Reply To All	Displays the RE: (Reply) form so you can respond to a message by sending the sender and all of the other message recipients a new message
Forward	Displays the FW: (Forward) form so you can forward a copy of a message to somebody else

Help Menu

Microsoft Outlook Help	Displays the Office Assistant
Microsoft Fax Help Topics	Displays the Microsoft Fax Help Topics dialog box
Contents And Index	Displays the Microsoft Outlook Help Topics dialog box
What's This?	Adds a question mark to the pointer, and displays an explanatory pop-up message the next time you click any item
Microsoft On The Web	Displays a submenu listing Web sites with useful information about Outlook
About Microsoft Outlook	Displays the About Microsoft Outlook dialog box and gives information about the available memory and system resources

Outlook Inbox Toolbar Buttons

 Displays the Message form so you can create a new message, or displays a drop-down list of other new items you can create

 Prints the selected message

 Moves the selected folder or message to a different location

 Deletes the selected message or folder

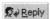 Displays the RE: (Reply) form so you can respond to a message by sending the sender a new message

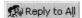 Displays the RE: (Reply To All) form so you can respond to a message by sending the sender and all of the other message recipients a new message

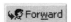 Displays the FW: (Forward) form so you can forward a copy of a message to somebody else

 Displays the Address Book

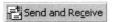 Sends outgoing messages and retrieves incoming messages

 Opens the Find pane so you can search for messages

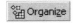 Opens the Organize pane so you can move messages or change views

 Starts the Office Assistant

Message Form Commands

File Menu

New		Displays a submenu of new items you can create
	Mail Message	Opens a new Message form
	Appointment	Opens a new Appointment form
	Meeting Request	Opens a new Meeting Request form
	Online Meeting Request	Opens a Meeting form for sending invitations
	Contact	Opens a new Contact form
	Task	Opens a new Task form
	Task Request	Opens a new Task Request form
	Journal Entry	Opens a new Journal Entry form
	Note	Opens a new Note
	Post In This Folder	Displays the Post form so you can place a post (or a file) in a folder
	Office Document	Opens a new Microsoft Office document
	Choose Form...	Displays a list of templates you can use
Send		Sends the message
Send Using		Allows you to select the service you want to use for sending the message (Internet Only version)
Send Options		Displays a dialog box that allows you to specify options for sending messages over an Exchange server or for sending faxes
Save		Saves the message in the selected folder
Save Stationery...		Allows you to save an HTML message you create as stationery, which you can use for creating other messages
Save As...		Saves the message in the specified location
Save Attachments...		Displays a submenu of any attachments to the message
Delete		Deletes the message
Move To Folder...		Moves the message to a different location

Copy To Folder...	Copies the message to a different location
Page Setup	Displays the Page Setup submenu
Memo Style	Opens the Page Setup: Memo Style dialog box to let you set memo style printing options for printing the message
Define Print Styles...	Opens the Define Print Styles dialog box
Print Preview	Displays a window that shows how the printed message will look
Print...	Prints the message
Properties	Displays and lets you change the properties of the message
Close	Closes the Message form window

Edit Menu

Undo	Reverses, or undoes, the last change to the message
Redo	Restores the last change you reversed when you chose the Undo command
Cut	Moves the current message selection to the Clipboard
Copy	Moves a copy of the current message selection to the Clipboard
Paste	Copies the Clipboard contents to the message
Paste Special...	Inserts the Clipboard contents or some portion of the Clipboard contents in the message
Clear	Deletes selected message text
Select All	Selects the entire message
Mark As Unread	Marks the message as unread in the information viewer
Edit Message	Allows you to edit the text of a message you receive
Find...	Looks for text that matches a specific description
Find Next	Looks for the next instance of text that matches a specific description
Object	Displays a submenu of commands relating to the selected object

View Menu

Pre<u>v</u>ious   Displays the previous submenu

<u>I</u>tem   Displays the previous message in the current folder

<u>U</u>nread Item   Displays the previous unread message in the current folder

Item In <u>C</u>onversation Topic   Displays the previous item in the current folder in the same conversation topic as the selected message

Item From <u>S</u>ender   Displays the previous item in the folder from the same sender as the sender of the selected message

<u>H</u>igh Importance Item   Displays the previous high importance item in the current folder

<u>F</u>lagged Message   Displays the previous flagged message in the current folder

Fi<u>r</u>st Item In Folder   Displays the first item in the current folder

Ne<u>x</u>t   Displays the Next submenu

<u>I</u>tem   Displays the next message in the current folder

<u>U</u>nread Item   Displays the next unread message in the current folder

Item In <u>C</u>onversation Topic   Displays the next item in the current folder in the same conversation topic as the selected message

Item From <u>S</u>ender   Displays the next item in the folder from the same sender as the sender of the selected message

<u>H</u>igh Importance Item   Displays the next high importance item in the current folder

<u>F</u>lagged Message   Displays the next flagged message in the current folder

<u>L</u>ast Item In Folder   Displays the last item in the current folder

<u>F</u>onts   Allows you to specify which font you want to use for reading messages you receive

<u>L</u>anguage   Allows you to specify which defined language you want to use for reading messages you receive

Message Header	Toggles between the full message header and the short message header
From Field	Displays or hides the From box in the Message form (Outlook marks the command with a check mark when the From box is present.)
Bcc Field	Displays or hides the Bcc, or blind carbon copy, box in the Message form (Outlook marks the command with a check mark when the Bcc box is present.)
Options...	Lets you set tracking, delivery, and status options for the message
Toolbars	Displays the Toolbars submenu
Standard	Displays or hides the Message form's Standard toolbar (Outlook marks the command with a check mark when the Standard toolbar is present.)
Formatting	Displays or hides the Message form's Formatting toolbar (Outlook marks the command with a check mark when the Formatting toolbar is present.)
Customize...	Displays a dialog box for rearranging the buttons on the toolbars

Insert Menu

File...	Inserts a file in your message
Item...	Inserts a message (from one of your Outlook folders) in your message
Object...	Inserts an object such as a drawing or a piece of WordArt text art in a message
Signature	Displays a submenu for choosing a signature to insert in your message
Horizontal Line	Draws a horizontal line across an HTML message
Picture...	Opens the Picture dialog box so you can insert art in an HTML message
Hyperlink...	Opens a dialog box so you can type a URL address in an HTML message
Remove Hyperlink	Turns a hyperlink in an HTML message into normal text

Format Menu

Style	Opens a submenu for choosing a style for an HTML message
Font...	Changes the font of the selected characters
Paragraph...	Changes the alignment of the selected paragraphs and adds or removes bullets
Background	Opens the Background submenu
Picture...	Opens the Picture dialog box so you can choose a picture as the background of an HTML message
Color	Lets you choose a color for the background of an HTML message
Language	Allows you to specify the alphabet you want to use for creating the message
Plain Text	Formats an HTML message as plain text
Rich Text (HTML)	Formats an HTML message as HTML rich text, which allows you to add character and paragraph formatting
Send Pictures From The Internet	Formats an HTML message so that JPEG or GIF images you include are sent along with the message

Tools Menu

Spelling...	Checks the spelling of the words you used in your message
Check Names	Verifies that you've correctly spelled the recipient names
Address Book...	Displays the Address Book
Fax Addressing Wizard...	Starts the Fax Addressing Wizard, which helps you address faxes
Forms	Opens the Message [Design] dialog box so you can design a custom form
Choose Form...	Allows you to choose which form you want to use for creating the message
Design This Form	Opens the Untitled Message Design form which you can use to create a new message form
Design A Form...	Opens a dialog box that lets you select an existing form from which you can create a new form

Publish Form Allows you to save the form you create

Publish Form As... Opens a dialog box that allows you to save the form you create under the name you specify

Script Debugger Runs the Script Debugger, which helps you fix errors in the scripts you create for custom forms

Actions Menu

New Mail Message	Displays the Message form so you can create a new message
New Fax Message	Starts a wizard that guides you through the process of creating a fax
Flag For Follow Up	Opens a dialog box so you can flag the form
Junk E-Mail	Displays the Junk E-Mail submenu

Add To Junk Senders List Adds the sender of the currently open message to your Junk Senders List

Add To Adult Content Senders List Adds the sender of the currently open message to your Adult Content Senders List

Find All	Displays the Find All submenu

Related Messages... Finds all other messages that have the same conversation topic as the currently open message

Messages From Sender... Finds all messages received from the sender of the displayed message

Reply	Displays the RE: (Reply) form so you can respond to a message by sending the sender a new message
Reply To All	Displays the RE: (Reply) form so you can respond to a message by sending the sender and all of the other message recipients a new message
Forward	Displays the FW: (Forward) form so you can forward a copy of a message to somebody else
Recall This Message...	Attempts to retrieve a sent message before it is read by the recipient
Resend This Message...	Opens a copy of the message so you can send it again

Help Menu

Microsoft Outlook Help	Displays the Office Assistant
Microsoft Fax Help Topics	Displays the Help Topics dialog box for Microsoft Fax
Contents And Index	Displays the Help Topics dialog box
What's This?	Adds a question mark to the pointer and displays an explanatory pop-up message the next time you click any item
Microsoft On The Web	Displays a submenu listing Web sites with useful information about Outlook
About Microsoft Outlook	Displays the About Microsoft Outlook dialog box and gives information about the available memory and system resources

Message Form Toolbar Buttons

Send	Sends the message
	Saves the message in a specified folder using a specified name
	Prints the message
	Moves the current selection to the Clipboard
	Moves a copy of the current selection to the Clipboard
	Copies the Clipboard contents to the Message form
	Inserts a signature
	Inserts a file in your message
	Opens the Select Names dialog box
	Checks recipient names

!	Sets the message importance to "high"
↓	Sets the message importance to "low"
▼	Adds a flag to the message
Options...	Opens the Message Options dialog box
	Displays the Office Assistant

Interested in what the Formatting toolbar buttons do?

I'm not going to describe what the Formatting tools do here. I already described them in the **Character Formatting** entry in this book.

Item-Specific Menu Commands

The Calendar Folder's Actions Menu

New Appointment	Lets you schedule a new appointment
New All Day Event	Lets you schedule a new event
New Meeting Request	Displays a Message form you can use to invite people to a meeting
New Online Meeting Request	Displays a Message form you can use to invite people to a new online meeting
Plan A Meeting...	Lets you plan and schedule a meeting
New Recurring Appointment	Lets you schedule a new appointment that recurs regularly
New Recurring Meeting	Lets you schedule a new meeting that recurs regularly
Forward As vCalendar	Forwards the selected appointment as an attachment in a message
Forward	Displays the FW: (Forward) form so you can forward information about an appointment, meeting, or event to somebody else

The Contacts Folder's Actions Menu

New Contact	Lets you add a new contact to your Contacts list
New Contact From Same Company	Lets you add to your Contacts list a new contact from the same company as the selected contact
New Fax Message	Starts a wizard that helps you create a fax
New Message To Contact	Opens a new Message form so you can send the contact an e-mail message
New Letter To Contact	Opens Microsoft Word and starts the Letter Wizard so you can write a letter to the contact
New Meeting With Contact	Lets you set up a meeting with someone on your Contacts list
Plan A Meeting...	Displays the Plan A Meeting dialog box so you can plan and schedule a meeting
New Task For Contact	Opens a new Task form so that you can send the contact a task request
Call Contact	Displays a submenu of commands for calling contacts
Call Using NetMeeting	Opens NetMeeting and initiates a call with the contact
Flag For Follow Up...	Flags a contact for follow up
Forward As vCard	Forwards the selected contact item as a vCard attachment in a message
Forward	Lets you forward contact information in an e-mail message

The Tasks Folder's Actions Menu

New Task	Lets you add a new task to your Tasks list
New Task Request	Lets you send a message requesting a task be performed
Save Task Order	Saves the order of the current Tasks list
Forward	Lets you forward information about a task in an e-mail message

E

F

N

O

The manuscript for this book was prepared and submitted to Microsoft Press in electronic form. Text files were prepared using Microsoft Word 97. Pages were composed by Stephen L. Nelson, Inc., using PageMaker 6.01 for Windows, with text in Minion and display type in Univers. Composed pages were delivered to the printer as electronic prepress files.

Cover Designer
Gregory Hickman

Interior Text Designer
Kim Eggleston

Page Layout, Illustration
Stefan Knorr

Editor
Paula Thurman

Writers
Stephen Nelson and Peter Weverka

Technical Editor
Kaarin Dolliver

Indexer
Julie Kawabata

Printed on recycled paper stock.